THE PRACTICAL TURN IN
POLITICAL THEORY

To Lea and Elias who fill our lives with so much joy

THE PRACTICAL TURN IN POLITICAL THEORY

Eva Erman and Niklas Möller

EDINBURGH
University Press

Edinburgh University Press is one of the leading university presses in the UK. We publish academic books and journals in our selected subject areas across the humanities and social sciences, combining cutting-edge scholarship with high editorial and production values to produce academic works of lasting importance. For more information visit our website: edinburghuniversitypress.com

Edinburgh University Press Ltd
The Tun – Holyrood Road,
12(2f) Jackson's Entry,
Edinburgh EH8 8PJ

Typeset in 11/13 Palatino LT Std by
IDSUK (DataConnection) Ltd

A CIP record for this book is available from the British Library

ISBN 978-1-4744-2543-8 (hardback)
ISBN 978-1-4744-2545-2 (webready PDF)
ISBN 978-1-4744-2546-9 (epub)

CONTENTS

ACKNOWLEDGEMENTS

Every researcher knows that the research process is a fundamentally dialogical exercise; this book is no exception. It has evolved through numerous discussions with friends and colleagues. We owe special thanks to John Cantwell, Thomas Christiano, Rainer Forst, Bob Goodin, Hallvard Lillehammer, Terry Macdonald, Enzo Rossi, Tor Sandqvist, Andrea Sangiovanni and Laura Valentini. We are always and forever grateful to Britt Erman for her help with the English language, which is a constant struggle for us non-native speakers. We also wish to thank the Prague critical theory crowd for the valuable feedback, in particular Jean Cohen, Maeve Cooke, Alessandro Ferrara, Nancy Fraser, María Pía Lara, David Rasmussen and Bill Scheuerman. In addition, Eva thanks the Swedish Research Council as well as Marianne and Marcus Wallenberg Foundation for the generous funding of her research. She also thanks Åke Wiberg Foundation for support of this book project.

Chapter 1

INTRODUCTION

All normative political principles are both shaped in and applied to social and political practices. How we best understand the relationship between practices and principles is a question of paramount importance that has always puzzled political theorists. Today, few would deny that current social and political practices play a role in deciding how best to realise, for example, a principle of justice or a principle of democracy. The presumption that the kind of political institution and the context in which the principle operates matter significantly for how we implement it largely permeates all areas of policy-making. In development assistance policy, for example, it is stressed time and again that the aid-giving country should avoid taking its own democratic system as an exportable blueprint when building democratic institutions in the receiving country.

Much more contested is whether social and political practices also should play a role in the very justification of normative political principles. To return to the aid example, it is heavily disputed whether and to what extent principles of democracy in the receiving country should be local and context bound. In the last couple of years, this question has received renewed attention in several debates in political theory. From disparate quarters, criticism has been directed at mainstream political theory for neglecting the importance of practices for theorising proper principles and for being too detached from real-world circumstances to be of any use. Several current debates bear witness to this discontent, taking the form of a criticism of so-called 'ideal theory' from 'non-ideal theory', of 'practice-independent theory' from 'practice-dependent theory', of 'political moralism' from 'political realism', and of mainstream liberal theory from 'pragmatist political theory' and 'pragmatist epistemic theory'.

These five debates focus on different values (e.g. justice, democracy and political legitimacy) and on different aspects of how social and political practices matter for normative theorising (e.g. for methodological reasons, epistemological reasons and political reasons), and have largely taken place in isolation from each other. The latter is unfortunate given that they not only address the same fundamental question of how social and political practices relate to normative political principles, but also share the assumption that practices in different ways *constrain* principles. This assumption is controversial, but has thus far escaped systematic scrutiny in political theory. To fill this void, the present book offers a comprehensive analysis of the claim that social and political practices constrain normative political principles. It will show that several of the specific problems addressed in each of these debates can be traced to shared general problems concerning the relationship between practices and principles. In doing so, it aspires to push political theory forward, engaging with and cross-fertilising key debates in the current theoretical literature.

WHY THE RENEWED INTEREST IN PRACTICES?

The question of what role social and political practices should play in the justification of normative political principles has accompanied political theory and philosophy from their birth. Among the Ancient Greek philosophers, Plato famously stressed that we should search for solutions to our political problems in men as they should be, rather than as they are. And while Socrates and Protagoras disagreed on most things, they agreed that we need a method or science for systematising and ordering our moral and political reasoning and deliberation, because people in their everyday practices tend to think about right and wrong in confused and unsystematic ways (Nussbaum 1986). By contrast, Machiavelli claimed that the Prince must rule in a world where men behave as they do, rather than in some ideal world where they behave as they ought to (Machiavelli 1961). Interestingly, Rousseau aspired to reconcile these strands in his search for a legitimate civil order. In his view, the Sovereign was the solution, according to which the legitimate principle of government takes 'men as they are and laws as they might be' (Rousseau 1997).

Why, one might wonder, are so many current debates in political theory focused on the role of practices for the justification of principles?

Given that this question has been of central concern since the infancy of political theory, it might seem moot. That is far from the case, however, and it is noteworthy that the interest has intensified so much in the last decade. Rather than being driven by sheer curiosity, an important source of this renewed interest seems to be a disapproval of mainstream liberal theory, typically defended by Western (often male) scholars, which has dominated and almost defined political theory. Most importantly, critics have voiced the concern that mainstream theory consists of armchair theorising and therefore is too detached from reality to guide political action and have any practical import.

In the debate on ideal and non-ideal theory, which has largely taken place within a Rawlsian paradigm, non-ideal theorists have been sceptical of the use of idealisations such as 'full compliance' when construing normative political principles, asking what they can tell us about how to act in circumstances of partial compliance. They have also questioned the usefulness of utopian theories, such as accounts of perfect justice, as they do not seem equipped to give much guidance in how they are to be realised from where we are now. In the debate on practice-independence and practice-dependence, practice-dependent theorists have raised doubts about the viability of mainstream theories, which do not take into account the nature of the practice to which a normative political principle is supposed to apply. In the debate on political moralism and political realism, the critique has taken the form of an anti-moralism. Political realists accuse political moralists of wrongly regarding normative political theory as applied ethics, such that moral principles are simply applied to political matters. A similar scepticism has been expressed by political theorists influenced by pragmatist theories of language and meaning – who we will call 'pragmatist political theorists' in the book – against mainstream liberal accounts, which are seen as too moralist and universalist to be able to address the challenges that pluralism raises in today's societies. Moreover, in the debate on the justification of democracy, political theorists influenced by American pragmatism – who we will call 'pragmatist epistemic theorists' in the book – have criticised liberal theories for grounding democracy in shared moral principles and values, which is impossible in circumstances of deep disagreement about moral matters.

Thus, a shared scepticism of mainstream liberal theory is indeed expressed in these debates. But while the renewed interest in the role of practices for the justification of principles has primarily emerged as a criticism, critics have not stopped there. Rather, in all five debates, alternative approaches to political theory have been offered, which not only stress the importance of looking at the workings of actual practices but also insist that such practices in different ways constrain normative political principles.

Starting out from this criticism, non-ideal theorists have developed alternative normative accounts, which are said to have practical import since they are able to guide action under current conditions. This has been done either by theorising what, for example, justice requires under conditions of partial compliance, or what a transition from where we are now to a more just state of affairs looks like. Practice-dependent theorists have suggested that normative political principles emerge because of the content and form of existing mediated relationships, which would not have emerged if these relationships had not existed. Political realists, on their part, have developed accounts of political legitimacy that are able to incorporate the constitutive features of politics, such as deep disagreement and conflict, by focusing on compromise rather than consensus, or by stressing the importance of the view of the majority rather than of reasonable agreement under hypothetical conditions. In democratic theory, pragmatist political theorists have developed alternate views of democracy, such as agonistic pluralism and aversive democracy, whereas pragmatist epistemic theorists have offered a justification of democracy which relies on epistemic principles that are claimed to be truly universal, rather than on contested moral principles.

THE ARGUMENT

This volume offers a wide-ranging analysis of the claim made in these five debates that social and political practices constrain normative political principles. The overall argument is twofold in that it consists of a critical claim and a constructive claim. The overall critical claim – the details of which constitute the main part of the book – is that the conclusions drawn in these debates about how practices constrain principles are either flawed or too strong. If true at all, it is only true in a much weaker form than suggested by its proponents. We analyse four kinds of constraints emphasised in this literature: linguistic constraints, methodological constraints, epistemic constraints and political constraints. With regard to linguistic constraints, we argue that neither the nature of language as such nor problems concerning shared meaning and understanding put any particular bans on normative political principles. About methodological constraints, it is argued that the interpretive practice-based method used by proponents in the five debates is invalid in its intended stronger version, and accepted by mainstream theorists in a weaker (and plausible) form. Concerning epistemic constraints, we reject that epistemic uncertainty either about empirical facts or about values necessitates a practice-based method which delimits our principles, as suggested in the literature. We furthermore argue that even if we accept certain epistemic principles as universally valid, as suggested by pragmatist epistemic theorists, they are not equipped to justify democracy, and thus fail to constitute a real alternative to moral principles suggested by mainstream accounts. With regard to political constraints, we contend that neither the constitutive features of politics nor the conceptual conditions of politics warrant the political realist constrictions on principles. Moreover, against the institutional version of practice-dependence, which presumes that the actual workings of currently existing institutions put limitations on principles, we show that given a strong interpretation, the thesis is unreasonable; and given a reasonable, weaker interpretation, it does not establish a distinct position vis-à-vis mainstream theory.

Our constructive claim in the book is that the theorist has much more leeway in construing normative political principles than suggested in the five debates that are scrutinised, and that whether (and how) practices constrain principles is a situational matter. Importantly, though, situational here is not to be understood as dependent on the practice upon which the intended principles are supposed to apply. Rather, it means that constraints on principles are dependent on what work these principles are intended to do, that is, what it is that they are supposed to regulate (and hence what problems they are meant to solve). We argue that the defended approach is flexible in the sense that it offers much more 'normative freedom' for the theorist than permitted by the accounts dissected in the book. However, the approach by no means entails no constraints on principles; we claim that practices do constrain principles, but not in the definite way advised in the literature studied.

On our account, two constraints on normative political principles are defended: what we call the 'fitness constraint' and the 'functional constraint'. The fitness constraint embodies the idea that the normative political principle must fit together with the other values, states of affairs and principles to which the account as a whole is committed. But the justification of this principle need not go from the 'bottom up', as suggested in these debates, that is, starting from the actual practices to work out the principle. It may equally well start from a higher-level principle in a 'top-down' manner. While the fitness constraint is a formal constraint on normative political principles, the functional constraint constitutes a substantial requirement. This constraint is set in relation to what the suggested principle is supposed to regulate, that is, what it aims to do.

The volume is structured as follows. In Chapter 2, we briefly present the five studied debates in political theory, bring up the main disputes in each debate, and review the grounds and concerns that are shared among the theorists. The subsequent four chapters analyse different ways in which practices are said to constrain principles: Chapter 3 analyses linguistic constraints, Chapter 4 analyses methodological constraints, Chapter 5 analyses epistemic constraints, and Chapter 6 political constraints. In Chapter 7, we discuss three general misunderstandings revealed by our analysis and how to avoid them, as well as develop our alternative account of constraints on normative principles in political theory.

THE CONTRIBUTION

In spite of the increased attention directed at the role of social and political practices for the justification of normative principles in political theory, research has been compartmentalised into sub-debates with little or no dialogue between them. While these debates have contributed innovative angles on several philosophical questions, they have also prohibited a comprehensive understanding of the relationship between practices and principles. To the extent that his relationship has been examined, it has often been done partially and indirectly, in connection with other theoretical disputes and in relation to individual theorists. For example, the criticism directed at ideal principles has largely been made through a criticism of Rawls' theory of justice. Notwithstanding the specific benefits that such a strategy brings with it (for example, in terms of concreteness), a one-sided focus on the specific account of a single philosopher, even if influential, comes with the risk of failing to take into account the underlying philosophical questions of a more fundamental nature about how social and political practices relate to normative political principles, which are paramount in order to draw *general* conclusions about the role of practices in theorising normative principles. It is such a systematic approach and comprehensive analysis that this book offers, by bringing together theorists from different debates in political theory into our analysis.

In addition, in each of the aforementioned debates, the core philosophical puzzles involved in elaborating the relationship between practices and principles have often been overshadowed by 'ideologically' driven contestations about how to best pursue normative political theory: ideal versus non-ideal theory, practice-independence versus practice-dependence, political moralism versus political realism, and mainstream political theory versus pragmatist political theory and pragmatist epistemic theory. This has resulted not only in overblown accusations between the different 'camps', but also to a deadlock concerning how to solve these puzzles and take the political-theoretical enterprise forward. The present book aims to offer a philosophically rigorous analysis of how practices may condition normative principles that eschews such dichotomisation, aiming to bring the field forward without an ideological superstructure. This is especially important since on closer examination, few (if any) theorists in these debates reject normative political principles as such, and even fewer deny the importance of looking at practices in theorising such principles.

The book is thus of theoretical significance since it advances the debates that currently dominate the field – concerned with questions of justice, political legitimacy and democracy – by pointing at joint problems of engagement, exposing paths that are not worth exploring and offering constructive ways forward. But it is also a philosophical contribution in that it generates knowledge of issues central to moral philosophy and metaethics, since it situates in a much clearer and more concrete context questions about the relationship between practices and normative principles, which are typically dealt with only in the abstract in the philosophical literature. Finally, our hope is that the book will also be practically important for empiricists because it provides conceptual and normative tools for studying real-world dilemmas, not least pertaining to policy-making of a globalised nature cutting across nation-state boundaries, which is characterised by large discrepancies between international demands for institutional reform and local social and political practices. Transnational policy-making has a tendency to become a heated process precisely because the normative principles underlying the policy suggestions are perceived by some participants involved as very far from their everyday practices.

Chapter 2

PRACTICES AND PRINCIPLES IN CURRENT DEBATES

This chapter surveys the renewed interest in social and political practices in recent years' political theory and situates the overall research question dealt with in the book – What role should social and political practices play in the justification of normative political principles? – in five current debates in political theory. It describes the main controversies in each debate, discusses the common grounds and concerns that have motivated the volume, as well as gives examples of the different kinds of constraints on principles suggested in this literature, which will be treated in detail in Chapters 3–6.

THE DEBATES

In recent years, an intensified discussion about the role of normative ideals has re-emerged primarily in the post-Rawlsian literature. What often goes under the heading of 'ideal theory', represented by liberal theorists like John Rawls and Ronald Dworkin, has increasingly become perceived as suspicious by so-called 'non-ideal theorists' (Mills 2005; Farrelly 2007). It has become a label for different theories involving 'idealistic' assumptions, such as theories involving idealisations, utopian theories presuming no or very permissive feasibility constraints, and end-state theories setting out a long-term goal for institutional reform (Valentini 2012, 2017; Rawls 1971; Cohen 2003; Simmons 2010). Non-ideal theorists maintain that ideal theory under any of those construals is too far removed from the concerns of real societies to be of much use in the real world. Instead, it is argued that normative theorising must be much more deeply integrated with the empirical reality of the society and that political theory at large should take much more seriously the non-ideal circumstances consisting of relations of domination and power under which normative ideals and principles are supposed to be applied (Erman and Möller 2013: 19).

Rather than assuming that people have the will and motivation to follow principles of justice, like Dworkin's theory of equality of resources, or assuming a society inhabited by fully capable adults living under favourable conditions, like Rawls' theory of justice, political theorists favouring non-ideal theory argue that we must carefully study the empirical reality of the society when we derive normative principles (Carens 2000). According to Colin Farrelly, for example, even more moderate ideal theories, such as Rawls' 'realistic utopia', are inherently flawed because they neglect the fact that trade-offs between values or ideal conditions unavoidably have to be made under non-ideal circumstances. Farrelly illustrates this with Rawls' priority of the liberty principle over the difference principle, stressing that even the enforcement of relatively minimal negative rights to protect people from interference are often very expensive in reality (Farrelly 2007: 853). Non-ideal theorists trace the problems of Rawls' ideal theory to its reliance on idealisations, such as full compliance. They ask how a theory designed under the idealisation of full compliance is at all helpful for understanding what is required of us in real conditions of partial compliance (Valentini 2012: 655; O'Neill 1996: 41). Also in societies like Rawls' realistic utopia people have misfortunes, and abstracting away such facts through idealisations only results in faulty normative prescriptions (Farrelly 2007: 855).

Hence, from a non-ideal standpoint, ideal theories are not only problematic because they are difficult to apply to real-world circumstances: they do not even hold as normative theories, since the prescriptions generated by their principles are erroneous. Non-ideal theorists, whether they are Marxists, feminists or critical race theorists, carefully study systems of domination and oppression as part of their theoretical analysis. A common assumption is that all theorising about morality takes place in a realm dominated by assumptions, norms and concepts that reflect the experience and interests of privileged groups in society. Therefore, the theorist has to be self-conscious and self-reflective about the concepts that 'spontaneously occur' when studying social and political practices, since these are the result of 'hegemonic ideational patterns' (Mills 2005: 175). Only by being aware of this can we formulate and justify appropriate normative principles and prescriptions, according to non-ideal theory.

A second debate analysed in this volume has arisen primarily in the context of global ethics, where the so-called 'practice-dependent' approach has gained attention. An important motivating force behind its emergence has been connected to the problem of scope in recent years' debate on global justice. A shared presumption among practice-dependent theorists is that the choice between a practice-independent and a practice-dependent approach has 'wide-ranging practical implications' for the scope of justice (Sangiovanni 2008: 140; Ronzoni 2009: 245–6). Generally, practice-dependent theorists are sceptical of cosmopolitan theories and defend statist or internationalist principles of justice in the global domain. The basic practice-dependent idea is that social practices and institutions fundamentally alter relations between people, and, consequently, the first principles of justice appropriate for them (Sangiovanni 2008; Ronzoni 2009; Banai et al. 2011; James 2005, 2012).

According to practice-dependent theorists, mainstream practice-independent theorists such as G. A. Cohen (2003, 2008) and Simon Caney (2005) neglect that the social or political practice to which a principle of justice is supposed to apply fundamentally affects the content and justification of that principle. By contrast, practice-dependent theorists claim that a principle of justice *depends* on the practice it is supposed to regulate (Sangiovanni 2008; Ronzoni 2009; Banai et al. 2011; James 2005; Rossi 2012). This is captured by Andrea Sangiovanni's so-called 'practice-dependence thesis', which is widely accepted among practice-dependent theorists, stating that 'the content, scope, and justification of a conception of justice depend on the structure and form of the practices that the conception is intended to govern' (Sangiovanni 2008: 138; see also Banai et al. 2011: 49; James 2005: 283–4, 2012: 30; Rossi 2012: 159). Intimately connected to this thesis is an interpretive methodology for deriving principles of justice from facts about existing practices, in particular regarding their point and purpose. Practice-dependent theorists argue that the practice-dependent thesis and the interpretive methodology together lead to different principles of justice from those suggested by practice-independent theorists (Erman and Möller 2016a: 4).

In current literatures, a third debate of interest in view of the overall research question focuses not on justice but on political legitimacy. Here, what goes under the label 'political realism' has become increasingly influential in the theoretical discussions about democracy and legitimacy. Political realists accuse so-called 'political moralists' of putting too much faith in abstract and general moral principles for justifying principles of political legitimacy, arguing instead that we must start out from the reality of 'dirty politics' and regard principles of legitimacy as distinctly political with little or no grounding in moral values. Interestingly, those theorists who are called political moralists are often the same theorists who are referred to as ideal theorists and practice-independent theorists in the above debates.

The main problem with political moralism, according to realists, is the so-called 'ethics first premise', that is, the premise that gives priority to morality over politics and regards the political domain as subordinate to the moral domain, mainly as an arena for the application of moral principles. By adopting the ethics first premise, realists argue, political moralists overlook that the political is an autonomous domain with its own distinctive conditions, standards and normative sources. Therefore, the adoption of the premise leads to flawed accounts of political legitimacy (Sleat 2010; Bellamy 2010; Geuss 2008; Williams 2005; Galston 2010; Horton 2010; cf. Erman and Möller 2015a: 216). The implications are twofold: first, that political legitimacy is then seen as a pre-political value in the sense that it assumes that consensus is required before politics can properly take place (Rossi 2012: 149–64), and second, that it leads to depoliticisation, that is, to a view of the political domain as deprived of any real politics (Horton 2010: 437). Raymond Geuss' words 'ethics is dead politics' is often used to express this concern (Geuss 2008: 42).

The realist response to the first concern is that, when theorising political legitimacy, consensus cannot be achieved through a philosophical argument in a stylised and moralised choice situation. Rather than drawing on normative sources from an external moral standpoint, normative sources of political legitimacy must be sought from within politics itself. Since consensus, or better, compromise or agreement is the result of politics, it cannot constitute a precondition (Bellamy 2010: 412–30; Mouffe 2005; Sleat 2010; Williams 2005). The response to the second concern is that, by regarding political legitimacy as a pre-political concept, through which real-world politics is sanitised by external moral reasoning, it is impossible to offer a plausible account of political agency and collective decision-making, both of which are constitutive features of politics (Rossi 2012; Sleat 203; Bellamy 2010; Newey 2010). According to realists, any plausible principle of political legitimacy must be compatible with the constitutive features of politics. And politics is concerned primarily with the provision and preservation of order (Jubb 2015b: 921; Galston 2010: 408). The aim is to find ways to live together despite unresolvable moral disagreement and deep conflicts of interest (Jubb 2015a: 679). As worded by Horton, 'gaining and maintaining political power are integral to politics in any circumstances' (Horton 2010: 435).

The fourth debate of interest has emerged in democratic theory, where some political theorists have been drawing on pragmatist theories of language and meaning for criticising mainstream accounts of democracy and for construing their own alternative accounts (e.g. Fossen 2013; Mouffe 1999; Tully 2009; Norval 2006). In this book, we call these theorists 'pragmatist political theorists', for short. Apart from the unifying feature of making normative use of pragmatist theories of language and meaning, some of them would describe themselves as pragmatists also in other respects, whereas others would be better described as deconstructivists or poststructuralists (Erman and Möller 2015b: 123).

According to pragmatist political theorists, mainstream liberal theory, represented by, for example, Jürgen Habermas and early Rawls, is ill-equipped to address the challenges that democratic societies face today, mainly because of its false reliance on moralist and universalist assumptions (Habermas 1996; Rawls 1971). To demonstrate this, they make use of pragmatist theories of language and meaning, mainly the works of Ludwig Wittgenstein and Robert Brandom. Wittgenstein, for example, points to an alternative way of theorising about the political, which rejects the universalising mode of liberal theory (Mouffe 2000: 61–2). The normative source of this criticism is found in Wittgenstein's specific form of contextualism, which implies that our democratic thinking is always dependent on our particular life situation and culture (Mouffe 2000: 73–4).

One of the virtues of Wittgenstein's contribution, according to pragmatist political theorists, is that it helps us to value the rich variety of ways in which democracy may be understood. On this view, there are countless ways of studying democracy and no universal criteria available to make comparative assessments among them (Tully 2002: 547). The approaches to democracy that pragmatist political theorists defend, with their focus on the agonist and aversive aspects of politics, are allegedly better equipped to accommodate this Wittgensteinian plurality (Mouffe 1999; Norval 2006, 2007).

The fifth debate analysed in this book shares several features with pragmatist political theorists, since it is also a debate in democratic theory in which political theorists make use of pragmatist ideas to criticise mainstream liberal theory. Rather than utilising pragmatist theories of language and meaning, however, these political theorists draw on American pragmatism – represented by philosophers like John Dewey, William James and C. S. Peirce – to develop an epistemic argument for democracy which appeals to the quality of decisions generated by a democratic procedure (Misak 2008: 94). In our analysis, we focus our attention on those political theorists who utilise C. S. Peirce's pragmatism to develop an alternative grounding of democracy, which is said to avoid the problems that liberal democratic theories face (Talisse 2005, 2007, 2009a, 2014; Misak 2000, 2004; Misak and Talisse 2014). Since these political theorists focus their analysis on the epistemic aspects of democracy, we call them 'pragmatist epistemic theorists' to distinguish them from the pragmatist political theorists mentioned above.

The motivating force behind the pragmatist epistemic approach is a failure of mainstream liberal theory to deal with what Robert Talisse calls 'the paradox of democratic justification', which emerges because democracy requires consent among the citizens, on the one hand, but people inevitably and reasonably disagree on fundamental moral matters, on the other. For this reason, it is impossible to offer a moral justification of democracy that is justifiable to all, which democracy requires (Talisse 2009a). Rather than offer a genuine justification of democracy, mainstream theorists such as Rawls and Habermas only provide a defence of liberal institutions to those who are already committed to liberal values. For anti-liberals, such an answer is question-begging since it assumes rather than grounds those values (Misak 2000: 24; Erman and Möller 2016b: 450–1). Hence, those who reject liberal values as a normative source for justifying democracy are left empty-handed, according to pragmatist epistemic theorists.

As long as liberal theory tries to ground democracy in a moral principle of any kind it will thus face insurmountable problems, since any modern society is constituted by a plurality of incompatible reasonable moral commitments. Therefore, pragmatist epistemic theorists instead approach the question of justification by appealing to fundamental epistemic principles, which are universally valid independent of moral disagreement. Even the anti-liberals and anti-democrats who try to deny these epistemic principles use them in the very practice of doing so (Talisse 2009a: 122).

COMMON CONCERNS

Theorists within these five debates have different aims (theorising justice, global justice, political legitimacy, democracy and so on) and work from different theoretical perspectives. Yet, they are all concerned with the same fundamental question: what is the proper role of social and political practices in the justification of normative political principles? Moreover, they make several common assumptions in responding to this question. First, it is assumed that normative political principles are dependent on the practice which they are supposed to regulate, in the sense that the practice in different ways constrains or puts limitations on the principles. A second shared assumption is that a thoroughgoing interpretation of the practice in question is required in order to theorise appropriate principles. The two assumptions are intimately connected, because to respond to the question about how, more precisely, the practice constrains the principles, the theorist needs to do careful interpretive work examining the nature of the practice, such as its point and purpose according to the participants, the structure of the interactions between them, and what they regard as valuable with the practice. In the book, we will refer to these two assumptions as the 'practice-based view' and call its advocates 'practice-based theorists' to have a common label for theorists in all five debates.

As noted in the overview of the five debates above, practice-based theorists are all indeed critical of mainstream theory. What we refer to as 'mainstream' (or 'traditional') theorists throughout the book is a broad category consisting of those who practice-based theorists describe as their opponents when developing their specific normative accounts, that is, those that allegedly find these two assumptions unnecessary, or even deny them. Theorists labelled 'mainstream' include, for example, John Simmons, John Rawls, Ronald Dworkin, G. A. Cohen, Jürgen Habermas, Thomas Pogge, Andrew Mason, David Estlund and Simon Caney. Interestingly, Rawls seems to become a watershed here, being pulled in different directions in different debates (seen as a proponent of the practice-based view among practice-dependent theorists but as an opponent among political realists). However, in view of the aim of analysing the practice-based view, the most plausible interpretation of individual theorists is not of immediate interest.

Also with regard to the key concepts – 'principles', 'practices' and 'constraints' – practice-based theorists share several assumptions. Concerning principles, all five debates focus on normative political principles (or what is sometimes called 'principles of political morality') – such as principles of justice, political legitimacy and democracy – that are intended to specify how a practice should be regulated and how the participants in it should act. Other kinds of principles of general interest in political theory, such as evaluative principles (e.g. specifying what is good or bad), are not treated in these debates and therefore not in the book. Hence, although practice-based theorists often are sceptical of the abstract generalist and universalist principles defended by their opponents, they do not reject principles as such. And since principalism as such is not rejected, in pursuing our study we leave out an analysis of views in philosophy rejecting the existence of normative principles altogether (normative particularist accounts).

Concerning practices, it is interesting to note, given its central role in the respective debates, that the concept as such is not much discussed in the literature. But from what we can tell, in all five debates it is mainly used in a broad, commonsensical and non-technical way, alluding to the social entities about which we typically use the concept. Naturally, political practices, which may or may not be institutionalised, play a central role here. Moreover, for the most part, actually existing practices (or historically existing ones) are taken to have a special normative significance, as opposed to, say, potential but never realised practices.

An exception to the absence of explicit specification of how '(social) practice' is used in the literature is Sangiovanni, who distinguishes between Rawls' rule-governed use of 'practice', focusing on institutionalised social practices, and Nicholas Southwood's more allowing account, explicitly endorsing the latter (Sangiovanni 2016: 3). On Southwood's (and thus Sangiovanni's) understanding of the notion – which explicitly aims to be commonsensical – a social practice is a social phenomenon where there is behaviour regularity among the group of people participating in the practice, where, as a matter of common knowledge, there are (or is thought to be) pro-attitudes to this behaviour among the participants, and where these pro-attitudes (or belief thereof) are part of what explains the behaviour (Southwood

2011: 775). The basic idea here is that mere regularity of behaviour is not enough. The behaviour of trees display regularities but do not constitute social practices. The same goes for much regular behaviour of *Homo sapiens*: our walking, sleeping and eating, for example, are not social practices in themselves. And the fact that we generally have pro-attitudes towards sleeping or eating does not make them social practices, on Southwood's notion, since what explains them are not the presence of these attitudes but something much more primitive and pre-social. When, on the other hand, there is a *particular* eating behaviour – such as using forks and knives and plates in a certain manner – where the pro-attitude towards that behaviour figures in the explanation of the phenomenon, it constitutes a social practice (Southwood 2011: 774–6).

In the book, a commonsensical notion of practice broad enough to also encompass non-institutionalised practices will for the most part suffice for our purposes, but we think that Southwood's account is on the right track, and since it is endorsed by some in the debate (and the rest do not say one way or the other), we will use it as our official understanding of the concept. As will become evident later on, delimiting the domain is less important than understanding the *role* that practices are taken to have in the justification of principles, regardless of (the details of) their delimitation.

Concerning constraints, this concept is given a broad interpretation in the book to accommodate the wide range of positions in these debates. While advocates of the practice-based view share the idea that there are limitations on the content, justification or methodology of normative political principles set by social and political practices, as well as agree on the general direction of these constraints (feasible, closer to reality, etc.), the precise constraints they argue for differ in both content and form. For example, practices may constrain principles by determining the principles, conditioning the principles or making them meet certain criteria of 'fitness' (Valentini 2011: 404, 409; Banai et al. 2011: 49–55; Rossi and Sleat 2014: 696). Practice-based theorists furthermore differ with respect to whether the defended constraint delimits the 'input side' or the 'output side' of the principle or value: does the constraint supply a set of, say, premises or methodologies which the principle must adhere to (input side), or does the constraint determine aspects – or the whole – of the content of the resulting principle (output side)? Some constraints are said to do both, such as the pragmatist epistemic argument discussed in Chapter 5, which puts forward a set of fundamental epistemic premises all agents have to adhere to, as well as argues for a principle of rule-making (deliberative democracy).

PRACTICES AND DIFFERENT KINDS OF CONSTRAINTS ON PRINCIPLES

Apart from diverging views with regard to how the constraints are supposed to delimit the normative principles in question, practice-based theorists also differ with regard to what kinds of constraints are highlighted as central. The next four chapters of the volume (Chapters 3–6) are structured around these different kinds of constraints. They will analyse the different ways in which practice-based theorists from the five debates have argued for their respective constraints. Our aim in these chapters is mainly critical. We demonstrate that these arguments for the most part do not hold and that the conclusions drawn about how they delimit normative political principles are flawed or too strong. We also show that, if the claims made by practice-based theorists are weakened, and thus become more plausible, they would not be rejected by their opponents in the debates (ideal theorists, practice-independent theorists, political moralists, mainstream liberal theorists and so on) and hence there would be no theoretically interesting opposition between the different camps, as practice-based theorists claim.

One way in which social and political practices are said to constrain normative political principles takes a linguistic form. As noted above, attempts have been made by pragmatist political theorists to argue for linguistic constraints on principles through the use of pragmatist theories of language and meaning. In Chapter 3, these linguistic constraints are examined, including both strict semantic and pragmatic aspects of language. One argument for linguistic constraints concerns how the very nature of language delimits normative political principles. Pragmatist political theorists argue that mainstream liberal theorists must give up the search for universal and generally applicable principles; for a political theory that puts forward universal principles of justice, political legitimacy, democracy or the like misunderstands the limitations that our different forms of life and the linguistic practices within them put on our theorising (Mouffe 1999; Tully 2009; Gunnell 2004).

Another argument for how linguistic practices delimit principles has to do with shared meaning and understanding. Pragmatist political theorists contend that pluralism is an essential feature of language, such that we cannot expect a term used in one linguistic practice to mean the same thing in another practice. Since we are only able to understand a principle as situated agents, we must reject mainstream liberal theorists' attempts to theorise democratic standards in the form of abstract general principles. Democratic procedures are complex practices and both understanding them and agreeing on them requires that we first agree on the language used (Tully 1989: 188; Mouffe 2000: 67). Any claim to universality is itself based on a convention of a particular linguistic practice.

Another way in which social and political practices are supposed to constrain normative political principles is of a methodological kind. Methodological aspects of how practices constrain principles, treated in Chapter 4, are by far the most discussed in the current theoretical literature, not only by practice-dependent theorists and non-ideal theorists in the debate on justice, but also by political realists in the debate on political legitimacy. In the chapter, we analyse different versions of what we call the 'practice-based method', which is a specification of the methodological commitments accommodated by the practice-based view described earlier.

According to this method, we should start our inquiry about the content and justification of normative political principles in a study of the relevant social and political practices. Since these practices fundamentally affect the relations between people, they also affect which principles are appropriate for them (Mills 2005; Farrelly 2007; Sangiovanni 2008; Ronzoni 2009; Banai et al. 2011; James, 2005, 2012). Therefore, as we saw before, the practice-based view requires that we conduct a thoroughgoing interpretation of the relevant practices. This methodological commitment is often specified in terms of a three-step approach: the first step consists of reaching an understanding of the point and purpose of the existing practices in question (James 2005: 301); the second consists of gathering information about what role it is that a principle of justice is envisioned to play among the participants; in the third step, the theorist derives appropriate principles using the interpretative facts established in the first two steps as parameters and fixed points (Sangiovanni 2008: 147; James 2005: 282; Ronzoni 2009: 233, n. 8; Rossi 2012: 159). For political realists, for example, this means to start the investigation in the actual workings of political institutions, rather than in some higher-order moral principle, and carefully interpret the ways in which political power and political agency is exercised (Rossi 2012; Rossi and Sleat 2014; Bellamy 2010; Geuss 2008).

The chapter analyses both weaker and stronger versions of the practice-based method and the suggested implications for how they constrain normative principles. According to a weaker version, the method is seen as 'open' in the sense that it stresses the importance of starting the investigation in existing practices but does not see this as the only method for justifying principles. According to a stronger version, however, it is assumed that only by making a thoroughgoing interpretation of the practice in question may we theorise proper principles. All abstract elements such as idealised hypothetical cases or general principles are deemed inappropriate.

Charles Mills, for example, defends the stronger version of the practice-based method. He argues that using concepts and principles that belong to the ideal sphere, that is, concepts that are not based in any existing social and political contexts, are inherently faulty (Mills 2005: 173–5). The abstract higher-order principles defended by ideal theorists cannot offer the appropriate conceptual tools to capture what ought to be done to make the society more just, he argues, since they simply 'assume away' existing injustices. Instead of using what Mills calls 'idealised' concepts, such as 'justice', his practice-based method commands us to make use of so-called 'non-idealised' concepts, such as 'patriarchy'. Non-idealised concepts spring from the actual experiences of the participants of a practice and can therefore assist us in recognising oppressive practices and understanding what ought to be done about them. This work cannot be done by idealised concepts, according to Mills, since they neglect these realities (Mills 2005: 172, 176–7).

If methodological constraints have received a lot of attention in current debates, much less attention has been directed at epistemological aspects. Yet, in the last couple of years we have seen several attempts to utilise a set of epistemic premises in order to justify constraints on normative political principles. Such epistemological constraints are discussed in Chapter 5.

One such argument originates from the debate on practice-dependence and focuses on purported deficiencies in our first-order knowledge about the political domain. It is argued that uncertainty about central empirical circumstances of politics requires that we adopt the practice-based method discussed above, which puts certain restrictions on theorising normative political principles. According to Aaron James, for example, who theorises principles of fair trade for the global economy, principles of justice must respond to the problems of moral assurance, that is, the problem that human beings even under favourable conditions lack control over the minds of others and therefore cooperate in the uncertainty of what others will do. A reasonable expectation of cooperation must be available (James 2012: 114–15), and this epistemic availability can be reached only through a practice-dependent method (2012: 117). This means, James argues, that we cannot neglect the present international system of cooperation when analysing fair trade (2012: 14).

In the same debate, it has also been argued that uncertainty about values and principles puts constraints on which methods are viable when justifying normative principles. Sangiovanni has recently argued that when the content of our fundamental, higher-level principles is too vague or unclear to generate determinate prescriptions, a special practice-dependent method, which he calls 'mediated deduction', is required when justifying a normative political principle (Sangiovanni 2016). While technically a weaker claim than he has made in earlier writings, where a practice-dependent methodology was said to be necessary in all political contexts (e.g. Sangiovanni 2008), it is clear from his examples of what constitutes (what we label here as) value uncertainty, that it would apply to the principles of most theorists, with the potential exception of utilitarians. Hence, were Sangiovanni right in his thesis, it would have far-reaching consequences in political theory.

Another example of an argument about epistemic constraints is developed by what we have called pragmatist epistemic theorists. Stressing the failure of mainstream liberal theory to ground democracy in a moral principle of some kind, pragmatist epistemic theorists instead ground democracy in epistemic principles, which are universal since they are also followed by those who explicitly reject democracy. On this epistemic view, insofar as anti-liberals and anti-democrats are belief-holders and truth-seekers, acknowledging that they have beliefs and trying to aim at getting the right beliefs, they must abide by certain democratic principles as believers (Misak 2000: 46). More specifically, the argument is that a number of epistemic commitments follow from these fundamental epistemic principles, which in turn justify democracy (Talisse 2009a: 15). An example of such a commitment is epistemic inclusion, which suggests that proper believing entails a requirement to tolerate criticism and to open up to new challenges to our beliefs. This, however, does not oblige certain moral commitments. Rather, unless we take seriously other's arguments against our beliefs, we do not do our best with regard to the aim of having true beliefs, according to pragmatist epistemic theorists (Talisse 2009a: 124).

The fourth kind of constraint on normative political principles defended in the current theoretical literature is of a political kind. In Chapter 6, such political constraints are examined. According to practice-dependent theorists, for example, justice must be theorised from the workings of actual political institutions, since these institutions alter the relationships of those involved and therefore also the status between them; they alter the principles of justice suitable for them (Sangiovanni 2008: 138). Similarly, political realists focus on how politics in different ways delimits normative principles, in their case principles of political legitimacy. One of the main problems with political moralism, realists argue, is that political legitimacy is theorised from a moral standpoint 'outside' politics such that the demands of morality give content to the principles. By neglecting to adjust their 'prescriptions to the constraints of real politics, rather than the other way around', moralism both fails to understand what politics is and generates erroneous prescriptions of little relevance for actual political practices and institutions (Rossi 2013: 558; Jubb 2015a: 679). Instead, principles of political legitimacy must be theorised from 'within' the political, focusing on the actual institutions, practices and processes through which citizens address shared problems in their society (Rossi 2012; Galston 2010; Newey 2010).

One such argument for political constraints on normative principles takes as its starting point the constitutive features of politics. The idea is that any plausible account of political legitimacy must be delimited by these features. In other words, to become principles that we aspire to apply to the real world, it must be possible for us to view them as consistent with the constitutive features of politics (Sleat forthcoming). For realists, these features include the preservation of order through coercion and the exercise of authority and organised violence, and the aim of finding ways to live together despite deep conflict and insoluble disagreement (Jubb 2015a: 679, 2015b: 919; Galston 2010: 408).

Another argument for political constraints refers to the very concept of politics in justifying a normative account of political legitimacy. This is often done by utilising Bernard William's conceptual distinction between 'politics' and 'sheer domination', which is said to provide the normative basis for political legitimacy, such that no additional normative sources external to a political practice are needed (Sleat 2010; Jubb and Rossi 2015; Hall 2017). The reason that the distinction itself adds a normative dimension to our very understanding of politics is because politics is a so-called 'thick evaluative concept', similar to concepts such as cruel and brave (Jubb and Rossi 2015). Thick evaluative concepts are neither purely normative (like right or good) nor purely descriptive (like chair or sky). Rather, to understand their meaning we must understand both their evaluative and descriptive content. Consequently, since we cannot understand the meaning of politics without grasping its evaluative aspect, we do not need to refer to any additional values to realise that politics is distinct from sheer domination (Rossi and Sleat 2014: 693; Jubb and Rossi 2015: 455–8; Williams 1985: 140–2).

A third argument for political constraints focuses on institutions from a practice-dependent perspective. On this view, institutions do not merely matter for the application of normative political principles, but also for their content and justification, since they place people in a special relation that gives rise to principles that would not have existed otherwise (Sangiovanni 2008: 140). Thus, the practices that constrain the principles are not only supposed to be actual but also institutionally mediated. In line with practice-dependence in general, the institutional version claims that institutionally mediated relationships condition the appropriate normative criteria (Sangiovanni 2008: 147).

In sum, four different kinds of constraints are studied in Chapters 3–6: linguistic constraints, methodological constraints, epistemological constraints and political constraints. It should be noted, however, that there are no sharp dividing lines between these constraints, since practice-based theorists typically defend several of them simultaneously through the same approach or the same overall argument. Added to this, no explicit references are made to them as different kinds of constraints by these theorists. The differences are only elucidated through our comprehensive analysis. While some claims are easily categorised in the four groups, there are also cases that are less clear. For example, one justificatory strategy employed by political realists utilises the concept of politics. We analyse this as a kind of political constraint even though it could plausibly also be discussed as a linguistic constraint. Importantly, though, the substantive argument we make against it holds independent of categorisation.

CHALLENGES AND WAYS FORWARD

The overall question of the book, investigating what role social and political practices should play in the justification of normative political principles, is thus responded to through an investigation of four kinds of constraints suggested in five current debates. In each of these individual chapters, we try to show that practice-based theorists often

draw erroneous or too strong conclusions about how social and political practices condition normative political principles. This has led the
debates into a deadlock, which has done little to progress the answer
to this overall question. Both this deadlock and possible ways forward
are the subjects of the final chapter. The aim of Chapter 7 is twofold:
to offer a comprehensive analysis of this deadlock, and to develop and
defend an alternative approach to constraints in theorising normative
political principles.

On our analysis, three misunderstandings have contributed to the
deadlock in the current literature. The first is traced to questions sur-
rounding what we call 'justificatory direction' in normative theorising.
Many practice-based theorists in these debates, especially those focusing on methodological and political constraints, seem to hold that the
truth of proposition 'Q justifies P' – in this case, that the social or political
practice Q justifies the principle P – proves the falsehood of the proposition 'P justifies Q'. In other words, it is argued that if we can show that
a practice places certain constraints on the content of a principle, then it
follows that mainstream political theory (such as ideal theory or political
moralism) is wrong to start out from some moral principle and simply
apply it to the practice in question.

But this is a logical fallacy, which has made practice-based theorists
neglect the many ways in which the two propositions, 'Q justifies P' and
'P justifies Q', may give each other support, rather than the justification going only in one direction. The holistic method of justification,
commonly known as the method of reflective equilibrium, is not only
acknowledged by most mainstream theorists, it is commonly endorsed
by practice-based theorists, too. To explicitly endorse it not only avoids
the logical fallacy, but also opens the door to a much richer approach
to the justification of normative principles, be it principles of justice,
democracy or political legitimacy.

The second misunderstanding, primarily made by theorists focusing
on epistemological constraints, is traced to a conflation of ontological
and epistemological aspects. In the final chapter, we argue that the (often
unreasonable) *epistemic* condition, that a theorist is required to *know* (or
at least carefully interpret) what the nature of the practice in question is,
including its point and purpose according to its participants, and so on,
does not follow from the (often reasonable) *ontological* condition that a
principle is dependent on the practice to which it is to be applied. It is
argued that if we keep epistemological and ontological aspects apart,
a much more nuanced and flexible approach for justifying normative

political principles comes to the fore, according which we search for the best substantive reason for a principle in view of the specific problem or purpose at hand.

The third misunderstanding, found across these debates in relation to all suggested constraints, concerns the view of feasibility constraints in normative theorising in binary terms. At the heart of the criticism of mainstream political theory in these debates is a concern for action-guidance and dissatisfaction with what mainstream theorists have had to offer in terms usefulness, since their abstract general principles are often not feasible even in the distant future. Yet, in the critics' own constructive theorising aiming to propose practically useful principles, it is often unclear under what feasibility constraints the suggested principles have been formulated and justified. In Chapter 7, we demonstrate that it is a mistake of practice-based theorists to categorically dismiss any principles on the basis of feasibility concerns – in their case, higher-level principles construed under permissive or no feasibility constraints. Arguing against such a dismissive approach, the chapter defends the view that we should allow for the adoption of different feasibility constraints depending on what work a normative political principle is intended to do in relation to the problem it is intended to address. This view of feasibility opens up room for a more multifaceted approach to the question of the role of practices in the justification of principles, since it sees feasibility constraints in terms of a continuum between ideal and non-ideal theorising rather than in binary terms.

As we argue in Chapter 7, avoiding these three misunderstandings opens up space for a much more flexible approach to the question of how practices constrain principles. On our alternative view, the theorist has much more freedom in developing a normative account than practice-based theorists have acknowledged. Indeed, we think that in the abstract, there is virtually *no* set of substantive methodological or justificatory constraints that the theorist attempting to justify a normative political principle in political theory needs to adhere to. Rather, the constraint which always applies is a formal one, having to do with the relation between the claims and premises made in the account. In practice, however, the aim of the theorist is indeed to develop an account of a particular kind for a particular practice, with some particular feasibility constraints. In such (rather common) circumstances, there are additional, more substantial constraints which apply.

In the second section of the chapter, we defend, and discuss the limits of, two kinds of constraints on normative political theories: what we call the 'fitness constraint' and the 'functional constraint'. The fitness constraint is a formal (or non-substantial) constraint, which utilises the basic idea that the normative political principle argued for in a theorist's account must fit together with the other principles, values and states of affairs used in the account. The fitness constraint has a negative and a positive aspect. The negative aspect of the fitness constraint is what we call its purely 'threshold' function: in order for an account to be valid, the set of commitments it contains must be *consistent* with each other. The positive aspect of the fitness constraint is about justificatory force: the stronger support the suggested principle is given by the other premises and claims of the account, the more justified it is. The negative aspect of the constraint is thus binary, whereas the positive aspect is (typically) a matter of degree.

The fitness constraint is a coherence constraint which bears close affinity with the notion of reflective equilibrium, and in Chapter 7 we discuss similarities and differences between the two notions. In particular, we discuss the fitness constraint in relation to various ways in which an account may be justified, the notion of ultimate justification, wide and narrow reflective equilibrium, internal and external reasons, whether the fitness constraint should be viewed as a methodological constraint, and how it relates to non-normative commitments.

Our second suggested constraint, the functional constraint, marks out a more substantial requirement on normative political theories than the largely formal nature of the fitness constraint. The functional constraint involves the requirements put on a normative account due to what it aims to *do*, that is, what the principle of an account is supposed to regulate and whether there are any particular limits within which it is intended to do so. The functional constraint involves three key aspects: the principle-kind aspect, the practice-kind aspect and the feasibility aspect. The principle-kind aspect is the constraint emanating from the kind of principle the account is intended to capture. In political theory, this kind-restriction entails some substantial set of constraints as to the content of the principle. For example, a principle of justice for an institution is typically different from a principle of legitimacy for that very same institution.

The second aspect of the functional constraint treated in the chapter is what we call the practice-kind aspect, the constraint emanating from which kind of practice the principle of an account is intended to regulate. Whether the principle of, say, justice, is to be applied to the appointment of professors at a university or the leader of a family business arguably matters for the content of the principle. This aspect in particular has been brought forward as setting heavy constraints on the principle of an account, and we demonstrate how the extent to which this is the case is highly open to debate. Indeed, we argue that even the often-reasonable idea that the principle must be compatible with the practice it is intended to regulate is non-obligatory, and show examples of when it does not hold.

The third aspect of the functional constraint relates directly to the feasibility requirement of a theory. Feasibility, we argue, should not be viewed in binary terms, dividing accounts into those in which feasibility matters and those in which it does not, but is rather a gradual affair, strongly determined by the aim of the normative theorist, by what she is trying to accomplish. Rather than taking one 'level' of feasibility as the primary one, a multitude of accounts may be justified, but with different feasibility conditions. Among other things, this view of feasibility takes us to a picture of the distinction between ideal and ideal theory as two sides of the same coin, rather than the dichotomous picture painted by practice-based theorists.

Chapter 3

LINGUISTIC CONSTRAINTS

In recent years, the linguistic aspect of how social and political practices may condition normative political principles has been discussed. In several current debates, political theorists have been using pragmatist theories of language and meaning for normative purposes. We referred to them in Chapter 2 as 'pragmatist political theorists'. In this chapter, we examine different attempts made by these theorists to argue for linguistic constraints on normative political principles. Linguistic constraints are understood here in a broadly semantic sense, including strict semantic as well as pragmatic aspects of language.

It is well known that Ludwig Wittgenstein's insights have had a major impact on how contemporary philosophers apprehend the role of practice for understanding and meaning. But a number of pragmatist political theorists argue that Wittgenstein teaches us lessons not only about how language functions, but also about how it delimits normative political principles. Chantal Mouffe, for example, claims that Wittgenstein's insight 'undermines the very objective' of aiming at universal principles and renounces mainstream liberal 'claims to universality' (Mouffe 2000: 73, 62). Since rules are inseparable from the form of life in which they exist, liberal democratic principles or institutions 'do not provide the rational solution' but are only 'defining one possible political "language-game" among others' (Mouffe 2000: 64). Similarly, James Tully claims that Wittgenstein's rule-following considerations and remarks about 'family resemblance' demonstrate the futility of 'developing a definite theory' (2002: 542–3). Since family resemblances among uses of a concept change over time, 'understanding political concepts and problems cannot be the theoretical activity of discovering a general and comprehensive rule', according to Tully (2002: 542). Even John Gunnell, who has criticised attempts to use

Wittgenstein for political-theoretical purposes (1998, 2013), claims that Wittgenstein 'subverts the search for the universality of both politics and political inquiry' (2004: 77). He further argues that Wittgenstein's conventionalism has 'fundamental democratic implications'. Gunnell writes: 'If there are no transconventional standards of judgment, then the logic of some form of popular sovereignty and equality is unavoidable' (2004: 89). Hence, for these pragmatist political theorists, a normative political theory that puts forward generally applicable universal principles of justice, democracy or political legitimacy – in their view, most mainstream liberal theories dominating the debates – is seriously misunderstanding the limitations that our different forms of life put on our theorising.

While Wittgenstein is by far the most common example of how linguistic insights are used for normative theoretical purposes, he is far from the only one. Recently, several theorists have claimed that insights from the socio-pragmatist philosopher Robert Brandom may be put to normative use in political theory. Notably, Thomas Fossen has argued that Brandom's account has political implications (2013, 2014). Although his Brandom-influenced arguments seem quite different from those related to Wittgenstein's, Fossen's conclusions bear strong similarities to those of the above theorists. Fossen's anti-theoretic and anti-generalist conclusions share both the content and much of the same terminology with theorists such as Mouffe and Tully, for example, that 'the legitimacy of an authority cannot be determined with certainty, definitively, or from a disengaged standpoint' or that 'distinguishing in practice between what is legitimate and what merely purports to be so . . . is not an abstract question calling for a general solution' (Fossen 2013: 445–6).

In what follows, we will investigate whether the teachings of Wittgenstein and Brandom about linguistic practices really motivate the metanormative and normative constraints on normative political principles for which they are utilised by pragmatist political theorists.

WITTGENSTEIN AND METANORMATIVE CONSTRAINTS

Since Wittgenstein is arguably one of the most influential philosophers of the last century, it is hardly surprising that there is a large number of theorists in the political theory literature who are influenced in one way or another by his thoughts on language and meaning.[1] In this section, we investigate a number of distinct (if interconnected) claims about how our linguistic practices are said to condition normative political principles. We focus on three pragmatist political theorists – Chantal Mouffe, Aletta Norval and James Tully – who, albeit for somewhat different purposes, share a similar idea about how Wittgenstein's view of the role of linguistic practices for understanding and meaning conferral puts important constraints on normative political principles. His insights about language, they argue, steer us away from universal principles that apply to all, towards a focus on the changing landscape of politics in each individual society.

In Mouffe's view, Wittgenstein's insights are 'undermining the very basis' of the 'universalist-rationalist' form of reasoning that underpins the liberal democratic approach as a whole, defended for example by Ronald Dworkin, Jürgen Habermas and the early John Rawls (Mouffe 2000: 64, 73). Instead, Wittgenstein points to 'a *new way of theorizing* about the political, one that breaks with the universalizing and homogenizing mode that has informed most of liberal theory' as well as 'renounce its [liberal] claims to universality' (Mouffe 2000: 61–2). The source of this criticism, Mouffe argues, is found in Wittgenstein's specific form of contextualism, which allegedly teaches us that in order to have an agreement or reach consensus, we must first have an agreement on the language used, which in turn implies agreement on what Wittgenstein famously calls a 'form of life'. For this reason, a political procedure cannot be seen as consisting of rules created on the basis of principles (such as Habermas' principle of democracy), which is simply applied to specific cases. Rather, rules for Wittgenstein are always abridgments of practices and as such inseparable from the form of life in which they exist (Mouffe 1999: 749). So, instead of mistakenly presuming that there is a correct understanding of a rule that any rational person should accept, in line with mainstream liberal theory, Wittgenstein's 'contribution to democratic thinking' helps us 'valorize the diversity of ways in which the "democratic game" can be played' (Mouffe 2000: 73–4). To take seriously the fact that we are always held captive in what Wittgenstein calls our 'language game', according to Mouffe, means to become more sensitive to the multiplicity of voices in a democratic polity and allow them forms of expression, which is exactly what her own 'agonistic' model of democracy is able to accommodate. In contrast, mainstream theories are obstacles to this Wittgensteinian democratic vision since they 'by necessity, tend to erase diversity' in their attempt to establish 'a rational consensus on universal principles' (Mouffe 2000: 73–4; see also Erman and Möller 2015b: 123–4).

In a similar manner, Norval employs Wittgenstein's concepts of 'language games' and 'forms of life', but also adds his concept of 'aspect change' in her criticism of mainstream theory and in developing her own so-called 'aversive' model of democracy. Norval finds liberal democratic theory such as Habermas' deliberative model impotent, since it focuses too much on reason-giving, rational argumentation and procedures that are supposed to bring about desired outcomes, whilst it has almost nothing to say about subjects' political participation. In Norval's view, Wittgenstein's approach offers a way of understanding the inaugurating moments of democratic subject formation and the practices involved in its maintenance (Norval 2009a: 308), since it 'resists the idealized theorizing and disregard for ordinary political activities' found in much contemporary political theory (Norval 2006: 231). In contrast to mainstream theories, which accommodate an abstract conception of the subject tied to what Norval calls the 'cognitive model of the acquisition and accumulation of facts', aspect change is not about changing one's way of looking at an object, but about a shift in perspective that establishes a different *relationship* between objects. The crucial point is that we do things differently once we have experienced a change of aspect (Norval 2006: 237). And, Norval continues, 'as with language, so with politics' (2006: 243). Human voice is not a preconstituted mode of political subjectification, expressed in terms of reason-giving practices through a set of procedures. Instead, a person discovers her political convictions as well as changes political identification by understanding herself in relation to a set of wider practices, in which her political voice is exercised in a myriad of ways, for example through rhetoric, contestation, passion and persuasion (Norval 2006: 244). Being based on a model of rational reason-giving, Habermas' model of deliberative democracy is not armed to address these aspects (Norval 2006: 250; see also Erman and Möller 2015b: 124–5).

Tully also makes use of Wittgenstein's concepts of 'aspect change', 'rule-following' and 'family resemblance' in his project to develop a political philosophy 'in a new key', which for him refers to a public philosophy as a critical activity. In his view, public philosophy has the capacity to bring to light injustices and relations of oppression while simultaneously working as an emancipatory practice by giving voice to the oppressed and exploited (Tully 2009: 3, 8–10). It is a 'critical attitude' rather than a transcendental Kantian or Habermasian doctrine dominating mainstream theory, which can 'test and reform dubious aspects of the dominant practices and form of problematization of politics against a better approach to what is going on in practice' (Tully 2002: 537). Instead of taking a transcendental route, which presupposes that we can and must identify a set of general principles for undertaking this emancipatory and critical activity, we provisionally follow conventional boundaries as we try to reach an agreement on something in our language games of critical reflection, questioning and altering the rules of the game as we go along (Tully 1989: 188–9). Since all judgements are made within unique language games in which the 'testing of true and false, just and unjust' takes place, 'there are countless ways of studying politics and no universal criteria for adjudicating among them' (Tully 2002: 547 and 533). Even if there is no such fixed normative framework of higher-order principles or norms of the kind that is presumed by timeless transcendental (mainstream) theory, according to Tully, subjects are still free to criticise every norm (2009: 58). Once we follow Wittgenstein and liberate ourselves from the convention that we are rational and free only to the extent that we can justify the grounds of any uses we follow, Tully argues, 'we can see that there is a multiplicity of ways of being rationally guided by rules of use' (1989: 183).

Before we explore in detail the actual arguments made by these theorists, let us first respond to a possible worry of readers with sympathy for the philosophy of (the late) Wittgenstein, namely, that we misconstrue these theorists by treating them as if they are engaged in 'traditional' forms of normative theorising, often described in terms of first-order (or substantive) normative theory. Wittgenstein believed a large part of his contribution to be therapeutic (Wittgenstein 1953: §133, §254), and consequently these followers should be interpreted as putting forward 'therapeutic' or metatheoretical suggestions. However, while it is true that the theorists treated in this section seem to be sceptical of certain forms of first-order theorising, Wittgensteinian ideas are de facto used to draw substantive normative conclusions about the weaknesses and strengths of specific normative political theories. Without doubt, to claim, for example, that a normative theory is 'bloodless', 'misguided', 'flawed', 'mistaken', 'problematic' and 'undermined', as the theorists treated in this section do, is clearly to move away from a therapeutic and metatheoretical exercise towards substantive normative one.

SCEPTICISM ABOUT UNIVERSAL PRINCIPLES: RULE-FOLLOWING CONSIDERATIONS AND FAMILY RESEMBLANCE

The Rule-Following Considerations

Let us start with one of the most famous insights of the later Wittgenstein. In what today is called the rule-following considerations, Wittgenstein's target is the idea that a principle (rule) wears its application 'on its sleeve', like a Platonic rail leading onwards into infinity, deciding what is in accordance with the principle and what is not (Wittgenstein 1953: §218). According to Wittgenstein, such an image is a chimera, since a principle only has determinate meaning given a background practice or custom, a way of applying it that is implicit in practice rather than explicit in the form of further background rules (since this would lead to a vicious regress). Persons who do not sufficiently share the background practice – the web of shared facts about behaviour and sensations that Wittgenstein often calls 'a form of life' – will thus not be able to understand the principle in question (Wittgenstein 1953: §241; cf. McDowell 1984: 348, 350–1).

The most famous example Wittgenstein uses to bring home this point relates to the correct application of mathematical terms. Even the most experienced mathematics professor has only made a finite number of calculations, and so for each person, we may find a mathematical calculation that she has not previously performed. Wittgenstein pictures in his example a student who is taught addition by instructions and a number of exercises, which he solves to the great satisfaction of his teacher. But when asked to add 2 to 1000, which is a number larger than any he had until then encountered, the student responds '1004', and continues the sequence with '1008', '1012' and so on (Wittgenstein 1953: §185). The teacher complains he was supposed to add the number '2' (not '4'), to which the student responds: 'Yes, isn't it right? I thought that was how I was *meant* to do. Or suppose he pointed to the series and said: But I went on in the same way' (Wittgenstein 1953: §185). Wittgenstein then goes on to demonstrate that there is no independently available image or notion to which the teacher may appeal to settle the case, since there is nothing in the image or notion in itself that decides how it is to be applied. It is not the signs or utterances but the linguistic practice in which they are written or uttered, our shared form of life, which entails that 1000+2 equals 1002 and not 1004 (Erman and Möller 2015b: 126–7).

While we have not encountered a clearly explained argument among pragmatist political theorists for why these considerations would preclude universal principles, we suspect that the thought is this: Wittgenstein has demonstrated here that there is no token, nothing which may be written down, uttered or otherwise brought forward, which suffices to determine the content of a rule or principle. Given different practices, the same token may signify different things. And since we cannot 'isolate' the content of a principle from the practice, there *is* no universal principle. However, this argument is based on conflating two very different aspects: the *prerequisite* for understanding a principle, and the *content* of the principle itself, including its scope. Crucially, Wittgenstein addresses the former rather than the latter in his account: the point about how a linguistic community is grounded in a shared practice is about the prerequisite for understanding a principle or rule, *not* about the universality of its content. Indeed, this should be evident from the very example Wittgenstein uses to bring home his point, namely, the correct application of mathematical terms. Here Wittgenstein takes the very archetype of universal content, mathematics, in order to expose the idea of a rule entailing its own application as an illusion. But he does not in any way question that the rule for addition is universally applicable. He is not attempting to revise mathematics, suggesting that 'plus' means anything other than the universally applicable rule for addition that we are taught in school.

Of course, any mathematics student familiar with the notion of base (radix) knows that it makes perfect sense to claim, for example, that 1 plus 1 equals 10 if we are using the binary system rather than the more common decimal system. So given different background practices, the actual numbers representing addition varies. But again, this is not to say that there is something problematic with universal principles in mathematics. Instead, Wittgenstein's point is that a background practice is essential for the very notion of acting in accordance with a principle *to get any grip at all* (McDowell 1994; McGinn 1997; Lang 2001). Thus, the rule-following considerations are about understanding a principle or a rule – about the prerequisite of knowing 'how to go on' – not scepticism of there being a definite answer to what this amounts to. For this reason, they cannot be used to argue against the possibility of universal principles, neither in mathematics nor in politics (Erman and Möller 2015b: 127).[2]

Family Resemblance

Another influential thought captured by Wittgenstein – which is also claimed to preclude universal principles – is that there need not be any essential property that unites all entities correctly classified under a concept. In his remarks about family resemblance, Wittgenstein points to the plurality of things correctly classified as games – Olympic Games, board games and so on – and notes that rather than sharing some essential property in view of which they earned the label 'game', they seem to have *similarities* with each other – family resemblances (Wittgenstein 1953: §§65–71). Understanding the concept of game is usually a matter of grasping the complex interplay of similarities and differences that together constitute the concept, rather than knowing some set of necessary and (jointly) sufficient properties.

But just as Wittgenstein's rule-following considerations do not preclude universal principles, the notion of family resemblance also fails to establish such a constraint, *pace* Tully's insistence (2002: 543). Admittedly, it may rightfully be interpreted as a certain type of scepticism, but this scepticism is directed against the idea that analyses of meaning must – and perhaps even that they typically do – involve necessary and sufficient conditions for the application of terms, such that there must for example, be a definition of *chair*, which gives us a set of essential conditions for an object being a chair. But it does not imply that concepts *cannot* share essential properties. The mathematical term used in the previous example ('plus') seems possible to define this way. And the notion of family resemblance certainly does not say anything about universality. If anything, it suggests that principles containing terms that cannot be codified by necessary and sufficient conditions may be vague in the sense that it might sometimes be unclear whether they apply or not. But the fact that principles, however general, need judgement to be applied does nothing in itself to undermine the criticised mainstream theories of democracy and justice (e.g. Rawls or Habermas), however universally applicable (Erman and Möller 2015b: 127).

The erroneous conclusions about the possibility of certain types of normative political principles in view of rule-following and the family resemblance structure of concepts may be traced to a misconstrual of the *role* of practice – in particular the linguistic practice – in understanding and communication. It is hard to deny that people have to share enough of a practice in order to understand the meaning of a principle, norm or value, whether it concerns Tully's civic freedom, Mouffe's democratic procedure or Rawls' principles of justice. Necessarily, these accounts take form and get meaning *within* a practice – the practice supplying the *preconditions* for meaning with which Wittgenstein is concerned. But since the point that we would have to share a form of life in order for a rule to be intelligible applies to *all* rules (contextual, particular, universal, etc.), it is a mistake to believe, with Mouffe, that liberals cannot offer 'a correct understanding' of what constitutes a good regime due to the availability (in theory or in actuality) of alternative practices (Mouffe 2000). There is no contradiction between offering a correct answer and that the practice needed to understand it is only one among many conceivable practices. Hence, if Mouffe is right that mainstream theorists do not offer a correct answer, this cannot be the reason (Erman and Möller 2015b: 127).

CONTEXTUALISM: LANGUAGE GAMES AND ASPECT CHANGE

In addition to the negative argument against general and universal principles, pragmatist political theorists have envisioned more positive arguments for how Wittgenstein's view constrains normative political principles. Both the general idea of language games and Wittgenstein's thoughts on aspect change have been taken to push political theory in a contextualist and anti-theoretical direction. Below, we take a look at these arguments.

Language Games

Wittgenstein's notion of language games permeates much of his later philosophy. Closely related to his thoughts on rule-following and family resemblance, a language game is a set of more or less distinct, purposeful activities of situated agents, both linguistic and non-linguistic in nature (Wittgenstein 1953: §7). A linguistic practice consists of a myriad of such language games, each relatively simple activity 'consisting of language and the actions into which it is woven' (1953: §7). The multitude of language games in place in each larger linguistic practice makes pluralism an essential feature of language. Each language game gives rise to a logic of its own, creating norms about what it means to follow the rules of that game, and we cannot therefore expect different games to function in the same way. It follows from this that it is in the very *context* in which we, as agents, are situated that every formulated principle must be interpreted. The terms used in one language game can signify something else in another (Tully 2011; Mouffe 2000; Norval 2009b).

So far so good. The problems arise when pragmatist political theorists use the pluralism of language games as a criticism of the traditional way of developing normative political principles done by mainstream theorists. According to the theorists discussed in this chapter, Wittgenstein's thoughts about the plurality of language games, and hence the context-sensitivity of language, lie in opposition to the idea that political norms have the form of general principles valid across many different contexts assumed by mainstream theorists like Rawls, Habermas and Rainer Forst. In their view, such principles are not compatible with our incomplete knowledge. For example, Tully accuses Forst of defending 'unquestionable higher-order norms' (2011: 147; cf. Forst 2011) and Mouffe accuses liberal universalists of defending 'the rational solution' in the form of general rules and principles (2000: 63–4, 76). Given the diverse phenomenon of politics, the argument goes, we simply cannot expect to find reasons for one single set of principles of justice or legitimacy. Appreciating the pluralistic nature of language means to move away from such context-free accounts of normative principles. According to Tully, Wittgenstein teaches us that 'actual criteria for the application of a general political term are too various, indeterminate, and hence open to unpredictable extension to be explicated in terms of an implicit or transcendental set of rules or theory' (2002: 543).

However, this critique relies on a false dichotomy between contextual rules or principles (read: good) and general or universal rules or principles (read: bad), which is not motivated by the endorsement of the multitude of language games in linguistic practices. The main idea underlying the reasoning seems to be that since general principles suggested by mainstream theorists are context-free, they fail to apply to a particular language game constituting a specific political context.

Instead, we must construct context-specific rules for particular societies with their particular language games. But it cannot be that general principles are context-free and require additional judgement whereas context-sensitive principles already come with a full context and without the need for judgements in application. As Wittgenstein has taught us, *all* principles require judgement when they are to be applied. All actual decision situations are descriptively open-ended and for every principle, however contextual, we will always have to use judgement to apply it in a situation. In other words, pointing to context-sensitivity does not settle the matter (Erman and Möller 2015b: 129, 2013).

Moreover, for most political theorists, contextual information about, say, the aims and values of citizens and the actual workings of institutions are important pieces of input when theorising which principles ought to govern a particular society (see Chapter 4 on reflective equilibrium). In fact, the insight that the context matters for what we should do is also a basic premise in moral philosophy, which is typically viewed as paradigmatically universalistic (Erman and Möller 2015a; cf. Hooker and Little 2000). Furthermore, moral theorists have long stressed the need for judgement in application. Even Kant, the father of universal principles, was well aware that no matter how complete and convincing a normative theory might be, it cannot offer an immediate link between principle and application. The application of normative principles requires assessments, judgements and possible trade-offs in light of the specific social context in which the action is supposed to take place (Kant 1970). In other words, it is an explicitly stressed property of normative principles that they do not 'apply themselves' (Mill 1998; O'Neill 1996: 78; Hooker 2000: 88). This is why theorists like Habermas continuously stress that an application of a high-level principle to a complex situation requires that the situation is described as appropriately as possible in all relevant respects (Habermas 1985: 244–5; Erman and Möller 2015b: 129).

Aspect Change

A similar, but distinct, argument against generalist principles relies on Wittgenstein's notion of aspect change.[3] Wittgenstein's idea of aspect change concerns how subjects are able to see things in new ways through contestation, passion and persuasion. In his elaboration of the notion of aspect change, Wittgenstein makes use of the distinction

Figure 3.1 Duck or rabbit?

between 'seeing' and 'seeing-as'. The famous picture of the duck–rabbit (Figure 3.1) illustrates that while we may perceive of this picture as a duck or a rabbit, we cannot make sense of this difference in terms of a straightforward perceptual story about two distinct objects such that the difference in the two experiences arise from or is *caused* to occur to us through the object in the material world itself (the duck–rabbit). Rather, it is better understood as a difference in how the subjects *respond* to what they see, in their particular contexts of perception (Wittgenstein 1953: §195). An unaware subject may simply respond that there was a picture of a rabbit, whereas a subject having seen the potential in the picture may exclaim that she saw the duck–rabbit *as* a rabbit (Erman and Möller 2015b: 130).

While overtly concerned with perception and understanding, prag-matist political theorists have taken Wittgenstein's notion of aspect change to have consequences for normative political theory. Norval, for example, claims that one reason why mainstream liberal and delib-erative approaches are not equipped to offer an account of democratic agency is precisely because they do not grasp that Wittgenstein's idea of aspect change concerns how subjects are able to see things in new ways through persuasion, contestation and passion. Aspect change is thus central for understanding democratic subject formation (Norval 2006: 229). The experience of aspect change is a moment of subjective assent that involves a process of identification – a picture grabbing hold of us – that cannot be accounted for by mainstream democratic theories. For it is not simply an identification, according to Norval, but an 'identification-as' (2006: 244). Since an identification-as is an embodied act of passionate engagement (for example, 'I am a demo-crat!'), we cannot make sense of it through the linguistic reduction-ism and rationalism of these theories, according to Norval (2006: 231, 238, 241, 244). She elucidates this point with Habermas' deliberative model of democracy,[4] which allegedly puts forward 'a bloodless con-ception of participation' *because* it relies on rational argumentation. Such proceduralism, she argues, 'forecloses the question of the iden-tity-forming ethos of democracy' since it 'presupposes that we follow the rules "blindly"' (Norval 2006: 239).

Now, it might perhaps seem as if Norval is simply using Wittgen-stein's theory in a therapeutic rather than a substantively normative sense (in line with our potential objection dealt with earlier). Argu-ably, this concern could have been valid had Norval been faithful to her commitment to use Wittgenstein merely to 'reorient democratic theory' towards a 'different set of questions and engagements' (Norval 2007: 3; see also Owen 2003). But this is not all that she does. When pointing to the flaws of liberal and deliberative theories as well as to the merits of her own aversive democratic theory, Norval clearly has normative pretensions: while the mainstream account, which focuses on cognition and reason-giving, 'rules out understanding aspect change' as well as 'forecloses' questions about identity-formation, these aspects can alleg-edly be accounted for by Norval's own theory (Norval 2006: 236, 239).

Utilising Wittgenstein's work in this way to show that linguistic practices constrain normative political principles, however, is precisely to overextend its reach. Insofar as Wittgenstein is right, Norval is cor-rect in noticing that the context matters not only for how persons per-ceive something in the world, but also for the possibility of perceiving something anew. Furthermore, it seems plausible to presume, as does Norval, that without any possibility of such experiences, the subjects involved would have difficulty engaging in a democratic dialogue. However, these are epistemological conditions for *all* subjects in *all* situations and say nothing in particular about democracy or democratic agency. It is equally true of a case in which a subject participates in a political meeting and discovers through passionate engagement with the other members that his ethnic group is superior to all others by 'identifying-as' a racist ('I am a racist!'). Hence, these general conditions do not offer the normative source for drawing any conclusions about the strengths of the aversive model of democracy defended by Norval or about the defects of mainstream liberal and deliberative models (Erman and Möller 2015b: 130).

In addition, these conditions do not lend us the normative ammunition to argue against an overemphasis on reason-giving practices and in favour of passion and contestation. Habermas' subjects would presumably experience moments of aspect change and identification-as – before, during and after their formulation and reformulation of reasons – similar to Norval's subjects, insofar as these are epistemological conditions for all human practices and interactions, including, of course, the process of providing reasons (something also pointed out by Wittgenstein (1979)). Therefore, we cannot follow Norval and conclude that it is when reason-giving comes to an end that 'the act of identification, occurring during aspect change, assumes its relevance' (Norval 2006: 241). Because so far as they are epistemological conditions, as Wittgenstein maintains, identification and aspect change are with us 'all the way', as it were. In fact, the only way for Habermas' deliberative participants to even begin to follow the rules 'blindly', to use Norval's terms, is to understand the context in which these rules apply (Erman and Möller 2015b: 131).

BRANDOM AND METANORMATIVE CONSTRAINTS

Let us now move from attempts made by pragmatist political theorists to constrain normative political principles by utilising Wittgensteinian insights, to a similar attempt using Robert Brandom, an influential contemporary philosopher of language and mind. More specifically, we will look at Thomas Fossen's recent attempt to theorise political legitimacy and the agonal character of the political, drawing on Brandom's work.[5] Fossen's socio-pragmatist account of legitimacy has a number of meta-normative and even first-order normative claims that bear strong similarities to the claims of the Wittgenstein-influenced theorists previously treated in this chapter, namely that normative accounts of political legitimacy should not be general, theoretical or definite, but based on lived experience. While Fossen displays substantial knowledge of Brandom's complex pragmatist project and manages to demonstrate the usefulness of adopting a Brandom-inspired terminology for describing the practice involved in contesting and endorsing political claims, we will argue that he is in the end guilty of the same unjustified inferences from the nature of language to substantive constraints on normative political principles as the other pragmatist political theorists.

FOSSEN'S BRANDOMIAN PROJECT

The central aspect of Brandom's philosophy that Fossen utilises is the socio-pragmatist perspective, which starts in 'doings' rather than 'sayings'. What participants *do* when they categorise an entity or make a claim is paramount. Typically, endorsement is implicit in the practice prior to being made explicit in the form of claims. Brandom's paradigmatic example is the conditional. He points to the case that before having introduced an 'if. . .then' locution, we may not express the fact that if A is the case, then B is the case too. But we may still in practice treat B as following A in the sense that, say, as soon as we endorse A, we immediately also endorse B. In addition, Fossen also takes on board Brandom's deontic score-keeping model, according to which each participant keeps a score on others' as well as their own commitments and entitlements. For example, Anna may be committed to the claim that it is raining outside, since John has heard her make an assertion with what he took to have that content. However, she is not entitled to that claim, according to John, since it is in fact (according to John) not raining outside. Such score-keeping is essentially perspectival, and yet, Brandom claims, it may ground the idea of objective conceptual content.

Fossen applies this framework to the political context and to political theory. From a Brandomian perspective, he argues, we start 'by asking what one *does* in *taking* authority to be legitimate, rather than what it means for authority to *be* legitimate' (Fossen 2013: 432). On this socio-pragmatic view, politics is understood as a practice of stance-taking, such that calling a political authority legitimate is to make explicit a political stance towards it (Fossen 2013: 428). The theoretical concept of political legitimacy labels the political predicament of distinguishing in practice between what is legitimate and what is merely taken to be so: 'the point of speech and action is to alter the patterns of commitments and entitlements subjects and authorities attribute to one another, convincing others to shift their stances and rethink their responsibilities' (Fossen 2013: 439). Furthermore, this view emphasises the contestatory character of politics and the agonistic character of social and political practices, according to Fossen (2014).

Again, so far so good. Just as with Wittgenstein's considerations in previous sections, we do not contest the truth of Brandom's socio-pragmatic account of language and meaning. As with most systemic philosophical accounts, Brandom's project is controversial (see e.g. Grönert 2005), but this is not our problem. We share an affinity with the project, and in any case, since Fossen's project explicitly utilises Brandom's account, it is naturally tied to its success. The problem for Fossen is that his claims do not follow even if we assume that Brandom's account is correct. For all its descriptive accuracy, none of the metanormative or normative (treated in the next section) conclusions follows from the socio-pragmatist characterisation of what goes on in claiming or contesting political legitimacy. Just as with Wittgenstein's insights about language, meaning and understanding, the aspects Fossen utilises are *general* characteristics and as such give us no *particular* insight into political concepts in general or the concept of political legitimacy in particular. As such, they fail to suggest any particular constraints on normative political principles.

FOSSEN'S LOCATION PROBLEM

A common complication with accounts that attempt to bring forward a new perspective on a debate is that they may be hard to place. This 'location problem' is certainly present in Fossen's account. Contemporary attempts to study political legitimacy may be divided into two camps: normative approaches within political theory and descriptive approaches within social science. According to Fossen, the task of political theorists has mainly been to justify principles or criteria of legitimacy, which establish what it *is* for political authority to be legitimate (*de jure*). He labels such theoretical enterprises 'normativism' (which is equivalent to 'mainstream', as we have used the term in this book) and contrasts them with sociological accounts, which instead attempt to describe the conditions under which political authority is *taken to be* legitimate (de facto). On Fossen's portrayal of normativism, morality is seen as prior to politics in the sense that the *de jure* question about what legitimacy is, is responded to by 'applying a particular form of moral knowledge', which comes in the form of moral principles and criteria that are supposed to tell us under what (necessary and sufficient) conditions a political authority has a right to rule (Fossen 2013: 429–30).[6] Further, normativists seek a 'privileged standpoint' from where to offer a *general* and *definitive* theoretical solution concerning *de jure* legitimacy (Fossen 2013: 432, 442, 446).

Criticism has been directed at this strict division of labour between *de jure* and de facto approaches to political legitimacy,[7] but according to Fossen, no systematic attempt has been made so far to rethink the concept of political legitimacy so that it accommodates both the normative concern for what is legitimate and the descriptive concern for what is taken to be so (2013: 427). In Fossen's view, this is exactly what Brandom's socio-pragmatic account has the resources to do. Through the use of a Brandomian framework, Fossen reinterprets the distinction between *de jure* and de facto legitimacy in terms of 'the differences of social perspective between practically engaged participants' (Fossen 2013: 428). On a pragmatist order of explanation, the focus is, in the first instance, on what speakers *do* (the pragmatics of speech acts) in order to explain what their utterances mean.

In Fossen's view, such a Brandomian approach will bring about an alternative understanding of legitimacy. The property that distinguishes the approach from normativist approaches and makes it a 'genuine alternative' in political theory is that what is distinctly *political* about political legitimacy is explained in terms of a *practical* situation revolving around attempts to rule (Fossen 2013: 434, 428). By understanding the concept of legitimacy in terms of the pragmatic role it plays in political situations, Fossen concludes that distinguishing what is actually legitimate 'is not an abstract question calling for a general solution' from a disengaged and 'privileged standpoint' (2013: 446), but something that must be settled provisionally through lived experience (2013: 445–6).

In view of Fossen's characterisation, we do not find it easy to categorise his account. As we see it, there are basically three ways to put forward a genuine alternative in political theory. One way would be to give a revisionary account that somehow dissolves rather than solves the original problem of finding out which political orders are legitimate and which are not, revealing for example that the very question of which orders are legitimate is based on some sort of mistaken premise. Even though Fossen 'bracket[s] the question of what makes a political authority legitimate' (2013: 432), focusing instead on how persons or groups *take* it to be so, which gives the initial impression that he has such a revisionary account in mind, he also takes quite a few steps to demonstrate that the question of what is, in fact, legitimate, remains and can be accounted for on his view. Thus, Fossen does not aim to be revisionary in this sense (Erman and Möller 2014: 488–9).

A second way would be to put forward a new normative theory – whether in the form of general principles or in the form of more particular, contextual claims – about which political orders or processes are legitimate. This is the traditional way of doing political theory, but it is not Fossen's way. Continuing from the bracketing remark above, Fossen goes on to clarify that he does not put forward any first-order normative theory in the traditional sense: 'this study will not provide direct answers to questions of whether and why authority in certain circumstances is legitimate or illegitimate' (Fossen 2013: 432).

Fossen's account corresponds to a third, more indirect, way of providing an alternative in political philosophy. Instead of dissolving the original question of political legitimacy or giving a new answer to it, Fossen aims to supply a new perspective on it which leads to a number of *constraints* on what a positive normative account of legitimacy should look like, pointing to a new way of going forward when theorising legitimacy. Fossen elucidates his approach:

> there is a reason for leaving [the answer to what makes an authority legitimate] open: the picture of political legitimacy that I put forward casts the political predicament as calling for various forms of practical engagement, rather than a theoretical solution. (2013: 432)

During the course of developing his account, Fossen puts forward a number of such metanormative constraints on how the theorist should view political legitimacy in particular, 'directing' political theories away from theoretical principles with broad – perhaps even universal – scope, aiming at making determined claims on what is in fact legitimate. But, we ask, is Brandom's theory of language and mind useful for such purposes?

THE WRONG SORT OF LINGUISTIC THEORY

In order to explicate why the inference from Brandom's account of language and mind to substantive metanormative constraints for political theory is too long a stretch, let us distinguish between three types of theories. The first two are what David Lewis calls *foundational* and *descriptive* theories of meaning (Lewis 1970; see also Speaks 2010). A descriptive semantic theory answers the question 'What is the meaning of this word?' whereas a foundational theory answers the question 'In virtue of what does the word have that meaning?' (Speaks 2010). Indeed, many theories attempt to respond to both of these questions, and Brandom's *Making It Explicit* is a case in point. Here, Brandom's main aim is foundational; he offers a socio-pragmatic account, which characterises when and how certain practices count as linguistic practices, and when and how performances should be characterised as linguistic performances (paradigmatically assertions). Apart from this pragmatics, Brandom also provides an inferentialist account of conceptual content, where 'propositions are what can serve as premises and conclusions of inferences, that is, can serve as and stand in need of reasons' (Brandom 1994: xiv). Both of these accounts are foundational in the above sense. But parts of Brandom's project include aspects that are best categorised as descriptive, in particular where he explicates various logical and semantic concepts such as the conditional, truth and reference (Brandom 1994: Ch. 2 and 5).

Admittedly, the border between these two types of accounts are not always clear, but this does not matter for our purposes here, since they are both to be distinguished from a third type of account: a *normative* account of a particular word or concept. A normative account of a concept is an account of when it is *substantially* correct, as opposed to *semantically* correct, to categorise something under a concept or term. Hence, the aim of a normative account is not to specify the conditions under which we are right to interpret a theorist as using a particular concept, say 'justice' or 'legitimacy'. On the contrary, the theorist who puts forward a normative account in this sense is assuming that the reader is already a competent user of the concept or term in question. The normative theorist is instead presenting an account of when the competent concept-wielder utters true rather than false statements. If she puts forward a theory of justice or a theory of political legitimacy, she would not claim that a person who is not using the corresponding term in accordance with her theory is making a semantic mistake as much as a substantive one (Erman and Möller 2014: 491).

Equipped with the distinction introduced above between theories that are broadly speaking semantic (foundational and descriptive theories) and those that are substantively normative,[8] we may explain why the inference from Brandom's account to substantive normative accounts in political theory faces an uphill battle. For the most part (we will analyse the exceptions in the next section), Fossen's account is a direct application of Brandom's foundational theory of meaning. So when Fossen says that we may elucidate explicitly claiming legitimacy in terms of implicitly taking-to-be-legitimate, or in terms of stance-taking, this is correct only in a sense that does not distinguish legitimacy from any other concept: we may replace 'legitimacy' not only with any *political* term but with *any term at all*. On Brandom's account, meaning is conferred by the practice in which our performances are to be found, and that goes for the natural kind of concepts that figure in our explanation of scientific phenomena (mammal, water) as well as mathematical concepts (addition, imaginary numbers) and even semantic ones (truth, meaning, reference). Consider, for example, Fossen's claim that a pragmatist approach suggests that 'we explicate what is political about political legitimacy in terms of the kind of social practice in which "legitimacy" is used in a political sense, that is, in terms of *where and how the concept occurs*' (Fossen 2013: 434). This is entirely generic, which means that we may equally well say that we explicate what is mathematical about mathematical subtraction in terms of the kind of social practice in which 'subtraction' is used in a mathematical sense, that is, in terms of where and how the concept occurs. Moreover, since 'political judgment' can be traded for *any* judgement, when Fossen says that 'recasting the predicament in a pragmatic way enables us to frame political judgment as an ongoing task that calls for practical engagement, rather than a philosophical problem calling for a general solution' (Fossen 2013: 442), it would suggest that Fossen has demonstrated that *no problem calls for a general solution* (Erman and Möller 2014: 492).

The upshot of this is that what perhaps looked like a reasonable (if unsupported) transition from how practice grounds meaning to how political engagement *rather than* theory is the solution when we focus on the political domain, turns into an extremely radical, anti-theoretical theory. Analogously to our above considerations with regard to the rule-following considerations, such a theory would come at a great cost, since the prospect for the generality of mathematics, logics and natural science would be undermined. Fortunately, Brandom is in no way making such sceptical claims. On his account, there is nothing problematic about making explicit theoretical commitments that are general in scope. On the contrary, *he* puts forward a systematic theoretical account of meaning and content – a solution, if you will – which definitely has general pretensions. Consequently, Fossen has not shown why the foundational aspects of Brandom's theory imply any constraints on the generality of principles of political legitimacy.

The same is true of Fossen's other metanormative claims, such as the epistemic limitation that a theory of legitimacy cannot 'be determined with certainty, definitively, or from a disengaged standpoint' (Fossen 2013: 445) or the anti-theoretical and anti-generalist conclusion that 'distinguishing in practice between what is legitimate and what merely purports to be so is treated as a lived experience that can be made explicit in critical moments; it is not an abstract question calling for a general solution' (Fossen 2013: 446). We have already shown that Brandom's account does not preclude general theoretical conclusions, so let us focus on the remaining claims about determining something with certainty and treating the distinction between true and false claims to legitimacy as a lived experience.

With regard to the former claim, if not determining legitimacy with certainty or definitely merely means that we cannot have *infallible* knowledge of political legitimacy, that is, that it may turn out that even our best theory of political legitimacy is incorrect, it seems indeed to follow from a pragmatist account, since all knowledge claims are fallible on a theory such as Brandom's. But this is an uncontroversial claim about political epistemology that we suspect no political theorists would oppose, mainstream or otherwise. So with that interpretation, it does not put any substantial constraints on normative political principles at all. Similarly, if Fossen by 'disengaged standpoint' means a standpoint external to the linguistic practice, it is again impotent, since *all* political theorists studying legitimacy are presumably competent users of the concept of legitimacy (Erman and Möller 2014: 493).

If Fossen instead intends a stronger interpretation, according to which a 'disengaged standpoint' is a standpoint a person has if she is not directly involved in the 'critical moment' when a particular authority is first judged, it would indeed seem as if he has put a contextual limitation on the political theorist interested in when a practice is legitimate. However, it would be a limitation that is in no way supported by his account. Rather, it would be based on a conflation of the foundational theoretical question of how meaning is conferred through participants in linguistic practices in the first place (which of course is unimaginable without engagement in actual cases) with the different question of what is required for a participant to count as sharing the 'form of life' needed to tune in to the concepts thus established. Nothing in Brandom's pragmatist theory goes against the idea that a political theorist, although not standing on the barricades during some political struggle, is able to share the concepts necessary for being able to put forward convincing reasons for a particular principle of political legitimacy. On the contrary, the fact that she seems to be successfully engaging in that very practice gives us reason to assume the opposite, until proven wrong. And Fossen has not offered, or even suggested, such a proof (Erman and Möller 2014: 493).

FIRST-ORDER NORMATIVE CONSTRAINTS

A companion thought to the metanormative constraints treated in the chapter so far is the idea that the pragmatist perspective on linguistic practices brought forward by philosophers such as Wittgenstein and Brandom will lead to new first-order normative political theories. There are two main ways of interpreting 'leads to' here: causal and justificatory. The causal interpretation is not only hard to assess, it is also of lesser relevance in the present context. The Heisenberg uncertainty theorem may cause people to believe that, let us imagine, moral knowledge cannot be both fully determined and fully justified at the same time, without there being any reason to make any particular connection between a natural science theorem about the speed and position of a particle and moral knowledge. Interpreted as a justificatory claim, however, it really amounts to a first-order argument for or against certain normative principles in political theory. In this last section of the chapter, we investigate two examples of such first-order normative theorising.

BRANDOMIAN SELF-UNDERSTANDING TO THE RESCUE?

Let us start by returning to Fossen's attempt to use Brandomian basic thoughts in the debate on political legitimacy. As we saw above, Fossen claims that employing a socio-pragmatist perspective in political theory will bring us an alternative understanding of legitimacy. Here Fossen utilises both the general thoughts on core-keeping, stance-taking and the like, which we have already discussed, and a characterisation of political legitimacy which does not originate from Brandom (who does not talk about legitimacy at all), but is partly *couched* in Brandomian terms. The question we investigate here is whether the resulting account has the resources to lead to alternative normative theories of political legitimacy. Notably, Fossen himself does not develop such a normative theory, but claims that some recent approaches, such as those of Tully and Norval, take us a bit further on this alternative path (2013: 447–8).

In his account, Fossen focuses on political legitimacy when he turns to making substantial claims about the practical context of politics. His main suggestion is that the relevant practical situation revolves around the *attempt to rule*. Centring on this Weberian idea, Fossen enters into a discussion about different political expressions of power, concluding that '[i]nsofar as subjects *see* it *as* affecting their practical horizon . . . a form of power counts as "political authority" that "attempts to rule" (from that perspective)' (2013: 436).

It should be noted that here Fossen is moving beyond general socio-pragmatics into an account of political authority and legitimacy. However, it is still not a move to *normative* aspects of legitimacy. Rather, Fossen pinpoints when what we are doing is talking about political legitimacy rather than something else; a functional account similar to describing the concept of a chair in terms of what functional role it plays. Hence, it is no longer a foundational account in our threefold taxonomy of semantic theories, but a *descriptive* account of the meaning of political legitimacy. As such, it may help someone who is wondering whether what she (or someone else) is talking about is political legitimacy, or if the topic concerns something else. But it is still silent about when a political order (or action) *is* truly legitimate, as opposed to merely claiming to be so (by a political authority or by other participants).

Fossen's summary of his account further stresses how it focuses on the descriptive:

> The theoretical concept of 'political legitimacy' names a practical, political predicament . . . To take authority to be legitimate is to attribute to it an entitlement to rule and to undertake certain attendant political responsibilities (such as a commitment to treating it as a source of reasons). To reject it as illegitimate is to treat it as a coercive imposition. (Fossen 2013: 446)

As we saw above, on Brandom's account the point of *all* speech and action is to alter the patterns of commitments and entitlements of participants in the practice, and so the only part which goes beyond this generic characterisation and is specific for legitimacy is that the concept names a political predicament, that it is about entitlement to rule and that it involves certain political responsibilities; in effect, exactly the kind of general and broad characterisations we would expect of a descriptive account of the meaning of legitimacy.

The problem is that since the aspects of Brandom's theory that Fossen uses are foundational, and thus fully general, and his particular (descriptive) characterisation of the notion of legitimacy is conventional, it seems acceptable to *any* normative account of political legitimacy. Mainstream political theorists committed to normativism may thus perfectly well agree that the role of legitimacy in political speech and action revolves around the attempt to rule (especially since the term 'political legitimacy' is described by them as the right to rule), the justification of coercive power or the sanctioning of political authority.[9] They may also perfectly well agree that such attempts to rule, that is, such legitimacy claims, take place in political contexts through practices of stance-taking between subjects and authorities. For example, nothing in Allen Buchanan's alleged normativist account – which roughly states that a wielder of political power is legitimate to the extent that it does a credible job of protecting the basic human rights of those over whom it wields power (Buchanan 2002: 703) – would have to reject these pragmatist assumptions (Erman and Möller 2014: 496).[10]

The compatibility of Fossen's account to virtually all normative theories of legitimacy raises the question of why embracing it would 'lead to' new normative theories. This question is especially pressing since the Brandomian story that Fossen employs, while being seminal in the sense of offering a new way of *understanding* what we do (that is, how meaning is conferred through practice), is not telling us to *do* anything different from what we already do. If Brandom is right, we already, all of us, confer meaning through these score-keeping and stance-taking practices. So when Fossen discusses how important various forms of contestations are for disputing entitlement to authority, and points to the many forms they may take in politics – political ridicule, marching in protest, desecration of public symbols, and so on (2013: 438–41) – he is making explicit how *all* competent linguistic practitioners learn and develop their skill with political terms. And since this is what all of us already do in practice, in what way does pointing it out change our (normative) principles of what makes an order legitimate (Erman and Möller 2014: 496)?

As far as we can tell, Fossen does not say. The closest he comes to responding to this question is when he treats the potential worry that 'someone might grant all this about the political pragmatics of legitimacy, while denying that this helps us say anything about what is really legitimate', that is, about whether and under what conditions people ought to 'recognize or reject political authority' (2013: 441–2). The way Fossen depicts it, this worry presumes that the option available is a normativist theory of legitimacy, which assumes 'that the propriety of political stances should be understood with reference to a kind of explicit moral knowledge' (2013: 442). But this is not the case, argues Fossen, since he claims to have shown how the 'distinction between *de facto* and *de jure* legitimacy can be understood without reference to a distinct form of moral knowledge' (Fossen 2013: 442).

However, this is an odd way of outlining the worry. To begin with, a normative account need not have the normativist form of supplying general principles for when something is legitimate or not. As the particularist debate in moral and political philosophy has shown, normative prescriptions must not take the form of general principles, but may be fundamentally contextual, at the most taking the form of rules of thumb or defeasible generalisations (e.g. Hooker and Little 2000). Second, even if we assume that the sole form of normative theory is normativist (mainstream), the claim that it follows that 'the propriety of political stances should be understood with reference to a kind of explicit moral knowledge' is either trivial or false. It is trivial if it means that the theorist is supporting her account by explicit normative reasons.[11] Naturally, if we are to give an account of under what conditions something is legitimate, we need to give explicit arguments, which typically include references to values. But it is false if the claim is that the competent speaker must *understand* what is legitimate or not with reference to explicit moral knowledge. As we have already discussed, semantic competence need not be, and often *is* not, based on explicit knowledge. We are taught the meaning of most terms without explicit rules, and political terms are no exception. The normative political theorist is not objecting to the idea that a speaker, without any explicit knowledge of the underlying principles, may recognise that a particular authority is illegitimate, any more than the normative moral theorist is denying that a speaker without any explicit knowledge in ethical theory may recognise that murdering innocent children is wrong. The *task* of the normative political theorist, however, is to give an account of when an authority is legitimate – and this, as we just noted, includes the explicit giving and asking for reasons (Erman and Möller 2014: 497).

Moreover, Fossen's explicit treatment of the worry that his account does not help us 'say anything about what is really legitimate' seems toothless. Here, he stresses how the essentially perspectival viewpoint of score-keeping practices can make sense of the distinction sought between what is legitimate and what is merely taken to be so. So if Brandom's pragmatist project is successful, we have the means to explicate the distinction, for any X, between what is taken to be X and what is in fact X, such as between *de jure* and de facto legitimacy (Fossen 2013: 432).

But, again, since we have assumed for the sake of argument that Brandom's account is correct, the problem here is not that Fossen claims that the pragmatist account succeeds in making sense of this distinction. The problem is that it does not help Fossen's cause. Obviously, a satisfactory *foundational theory* must be able to distinguish between, say, someone believing it is raining outside and that it is actually raining outside. If the theory treats these two as one and the same, it is in trouble. But as a theory of the weather, managing to make sense of this basic distinction is of as little assistance as Tarski's Convention T is in finding actual truths. Understanding that 'it is raining outside' is true if and only if it is raining outside – or more generally, that any correct theory of truth must imply that the sentence 'p' is true if and only if p – may be great if our aim is to develop a theory of truth, but it does not help us to pick out truths in the world. Likewise, what Fossen puts forward is supposed to be a theory of political legitimacy. But if nothing is supplied beyond the pragmatics of legitimacy claims and the most basic conceptual analysis of the term, a foundational theory distinguishing in principle between *de jure* and de facto claims is of no assistance (Erman and Möller 2014: 498).

WITTGENSTEINIAN UNDERSTANDING, JUSTIFICATION AND NORMS

As we have seen, several of the pragmatist political theorists discussed in this chapter believe that Wittgenstein's thoughts about shared meaning, understanding and belief lead us away from mainstream political theories. For example, in elaborating democratic procedure, Mouffe argues against Rawls and Habermas that democratic procedures are complex ensembles of practices rather than rules that are created on the basis of principles. To agree on a procedure, she claims, requires agreement on the language used (Mouffe 2000: 67; cf. Habermas 1996). In Tully's view, resonating Mouffe's criticism, 'Habermas's mistake' is precisely that his priority of claims to rightness over other kinds of claims is itself grounded in a convention of a particular language game, namely the right in certain circumstances to ask for reasons (Tully 1989: 188; Erman and Möller 2015b: 131).

The line of thought displayed here, however, seems to conflate the question of whether a principle is *valid* with the question of *understanding* its content. To say that a person cannot understand a normative principle only says that she does not share the necessary preconditions, in terms of appropriate life world or language game, for the principle to become intelligible. To illustrate this, consider the rule, 'You should always divide a cake equally.' If the term 'equal' is understood in terms of merit in one society, such that an equal division means that people get pieces in relation to what they deserve, and if 'cake' in this society signifies petite madeleines and only petite madeleines, the rule means something different for people in that society from what it does for us. The possibility of agreement as well as disagreement about the *content* of a principle is premised if not exactly on 'agreement on the language used' (Mouffe), at least on the possibility of systematically being able to translate others' utterances.[12] But this commonsensical prerequisite on successful communication reflects only the *semantic* sense of 'agree on a procedure', that is to say, to agree on what the principle means. We can agree on this while at the same time strongly disagree about the *validity* of the principle. As long as we can grasp the statements of a speaker, in our own language or via translation, agreement on the content of a principle is possible. If 'equal' in the mouth of the speaker signifies 'merit' to us, we may understand that the linguistic item, 'You should always divide a cake equally', uttered by the speaker, means the same as the linguistic item 'You should always divide a cake according to merit', uttered by us (Erman and Möller 2015b: 131–2).

However, this says nothing about the validity of the principle so understood. The question of validity of a principle is in practice a matter of whether there are good reasons for it. And whatever our position is concerning theories of meaning, we are all in the same boat when it comes to the practice of justification. Being able to engage in such a practice is premised on the possibility of being able to communicate the content of the principle by following appropriate conventions (or by sufficiently understanding how the interlocutors' idioms deviate from such conventions). Indeed, sometimes this practice is undermined, but it would be a very controversial (and non-Wittgensteinian) claim to assert that communication about the propositional content of principles is impossible between different societies. While these Wittgensteinian linguistic insights set the limits for the discussion, they do not point in favour of any particular normative political principle.

This point has important implications for values. When pragmatist political theorists argue that the diversity of values following from the diversity of language games implies the futility of mainstream principles of justice and democracy, they again conflate two distinct concepts: values *held* and values we *ought to hold*. Indeed, it seems to be a commonsensical fact that people in different societies or cultures not only use a different language for expressing their values but also that the content, the held values, differ. But this fact does not entail either that they must have these values or that they should have these values. Normative political theory is foremost about how we should live and arrange our societies, and as with all (practical) normativity, it is an open question how and to what extent (current) facts matter for what we should do (Erman and Möller 2015b: 132; 2013; see also Chapter 4).

Let us illustrate with an example. Among the Hmong people, it is believed that children with epileptic seizures should not be treated with medicine.[13] This is a normative belief, which corresponds to a perceived value, namely the potentially beneficial effect of being spiritually possessed that they believe the seizures indicate. Now, we may acknowledge that the language game of the Hmong people includes references to spiritual forces and beliefs about their causal interaction with living people, and agree that *within* this system of belief, the value of withholding medical treatment for seizures makes sense. We may thus understand the beliefs and values of the Hmong people. But of course, this does not establish the truth or correctness of these beliefs and values. While the Hmong take there to be a value with withholding treatment, there is in fact no such value. The perceived value is based on erroneous beliefs (Erman and Möller 2015b: 132).[14]

Indeed, one tempting objection to this reasoning may be that here we are simply *presuming* that some – 'our' – beliefs and values are true or correct, whereas other – 'their' – beliefs and values are not, precisely highlighting the Wittgensteinian point that there is no neutral point of view, but only different language games, and different ways of perceiving the world and our place in it. The worry would thus be that the futility of mainstream political theory lies in believing that there is a transcendental standpoint from which we may prove that some values are true and others are false. However, this objection misses the above point about the validity of values. In arguing for a principle or value, we give what we take to be the most convincing reasons for it.

Of course, such reasons, be they factual or evaluative, are in turn based on assumptions, most of them implicit, and somewhere we hit rock bottom. Then, with Wittgenstein's famous quote, justification ends and we say: 'This is simply what I do' (Wittgenstein 1953: §217). But this anti-foundationalist idea of justification is in perfect alignment with the view of mainstream political theorists, who do not believe there to be an Archimedean point of reference on which we may rely. This is the entire point of a coherentist approach such as Rawls' reflective equilibrium (Rawls 1971, 2001; see also Chapter 4). And Habermas' determination to steer away from what he calls 'the paradigm of the philosophy of consciousness' is precisely meant to avoid such foundationalism, which in his view 'conflicts with our consciousness of the fallibility of human knowledge' (Habermas 1996: 193).

Naturally, in order to convince a Hmong that her non-treatment value is false, we would have to persuade her of the incorrectness of the beliefs about seizures indicating spiritual possession, which may be a very difficult task since we are potentially questioning an entire system of belief. But in principle, the situation is the same as when someone is convinced that drinking a glass of liquid is beneficial since he believes it is nutritious nectar, when in fact it is poisonous. Since truth is not transparent, when we say 'in fact', we are always implicitly alluding to something like 'according to my best understanding of how it is'. Indeed, it is exactly in that sense that we never move beyond 'held values' or 'held beliefs'. But a central point of making claims of value or fact *explicit* is to make them available for scrutiny, that is, for giving and asking for reasons. This may not be the only way to change people's views, but it is one important way (Erman and Möller 2015b: 133).

Consequently, while our justification always ends at some point, 'this is simply what I do' entails neither that it is what I must do nor that it is what I ought to do. Normative political principles may be questioned, but they may also be convincingly argued for. In this sense, Wittgenstein's point about the multitude of language games, and the corresponding point about forms of life, is descriptive rather than normative: it shows how language functions.[15] Successful communication is possible as long as we share enough of a life world. As long as this is the case, we may argue with each other about alternative ways of doing things. Most importantly in the present context, there is nothing in Wittgenstein's thought that stops the theorist from arguing that some ways of life (in this narrow sense) are unacceptable and therefore ought to be abandoned (Erman and Möller 2015b: 132).

NOTES

1. See, for example, Pitkin (1972); Rorty (1991); Gellner (1984); Botwinick (1985); Eldridge (2003); Pohlhaus and Wright (2002).
2. This is admitted by theorists who do argue against general principles in morality, for example McNaughton and Rawling (2000); Dancy (2004). Rule-following considerations is typically used to argue against the 'prejudice' of believing that moral rightness has to be codifiable, on pain of irrationality, as in McDowell (1979).
3. Note that the 'aspect change' discourse is clearly focused on conceptually mediated perception, that is, on linguistic aspects of perception. Whether all perception is conceptually mediated, as theorists such as McDowell (1994) believe, is a larger issue in relation to which we remain neutral.
4. However, she claims that 'Rawlsian accounts suffer from similar problems' (Norval 2006: 253 at n. 56).
5. For other recent attempts to use Brandom for political-theoretical purposes, see, for example, Springs (2009).
6. Typical normativists, according to Fossen, are Nagel (1991); Simmons (2001); Buchanan (2002); Christiano (2004).
7. See, for example the debate between political realism and political moralism discussed in this volume (Chapters 4, 5 and 6, in particular).
8. Of course, many theorists, Brandom included, take meaning to be a normative phenomenon (see, for example, McDowell 1994). However, normativity of meaning should not be conflated with substantial *practical normativity*, which is what is of primary concern in political theory and in this volume.
9. See, for example, Simmons 2001; Wellman 1996; Christiano 1996.
10. Moreover, in view of our argument above, the fact that Buchanan's account opts for a 'general solution' (Fossen 2013: 432, 442) is not problematic in relation to Fossen's account.
11. Whether such principles or conditions must be moral may indeed be doubted (see Williams 2005), although we have argued elsewhere that moral values do figure in the justification of principles of political legitimacy (see Erman and Möller 2015a).
12. For a famous elaboration on this, see Davidson 1974.
13. Of course, far from all members of the Hmong people live according to these traditional customs.
14. Note that this example merely questions the evidently fact-dependent value of withholding medical treatment, not the underlying value of doing what is beneficial for the person in question. To what extent we also disagree about more fundamental values is controversial; many theorists argue that much moral disagreement is due to different factual beliefs rather than different underlying values. For discussions on moral disagreement, see for example Gowans (2000); Tersman (2006).

15. That is not to deny, of course, that language itself is normative, as many theorists (ourselves included) believe it to be. The distinction we are after here is rather that between describing how and when to castle in chess. While it makes sense to say that you ought to castle by moving the king two squares towards a rook on the first rank, then moving the rook onto the square over which the king crossed, it is descriptive rather than normative in the sense we seek since what is described is simply what it means to castle – there is no alternative way for you to do it. In contrast, that you should castle early is a normative claim in the sense that you can do otherwise, although (in most cases) you should not.

Chapter 4

METHODOLOGICAL CONSTRAINTS

In current debates, the most discussed aspect of the relationship between social and political practices and normative political principles has been of a methodological kind. In this chapter, we examine this 'methodological turn' in political theory with regard to arguments made about how methodological considerations constrain normative political principles. As we saw in Chapter 2, such arguments have primarily been developed in the justice literature – by practice-dependent theorists against practice-independent principles and by non-ideal theorists against ideal principles – but also to some extent by political realists in the debate on political legitimacy. The problem of action-guidance lies at the heart of these concerns, but these critics also throw suspicion on the methodology used by mainstream political theorists. While coming from different quarters and working in different theoretical contexts, they share a number of methodological commitments. The aim here is to analyse the methodological arguments made in these debates as well as assess what constraints on normative principles are assumed to follow from these methodological commitments.

SHARED METHODOLOGICAL ASSUMPTIONS

There are a number of methodological assumptions shared by theorists in the different debates treated in this chapter. To begin with, practice-based theorists all stress the importance of starting in 'the actual' rather than in some general, higher-order principle when theorising normative political principles. Non-ideal theorists, for example, stress that general and higher-order principles rely on idealisations that exclude or at least marginalise our current world as it is, such as the workings of institutions, which leads to erroneous prescriptions (Mills 2005: 168). Instead of leaning on idealised (false) descriptions, the theorist should rely on facts about society (true descriptions), such as the permanent realities of partial compliance (Mills 2005: 177; Farrelly 2007: 859–60). Also practice-dependent theorists argue that we should take as the point of departure our social and political practices. They claim that practices and institutions fundamentally alter the relations in which people stand, and, consequently, 'the first principles of justice that are appropriate for them' (Sangiovanni 2008: 138). The nature of such practically mediated relations is such that it gives rise to principles that would not have existed otherwise (Sangiovanni 2008; Ronzoni 2009; Banai et al. 2011; James 2005, 2012). According to practice-dependent theorists, this is precisely what practice-independent theorists, such as G. A. Cohen and Simon Caney, would not accept (Cohen 2003, 2008; Caney 2005). While practice-independent theorists can allow for facts about human beings as such to enter into the justification of principles, they would deny that the same is true of empirical and interpretive facts about social practices and institutions (Sangiovanni 2008: 140). In a similar fashion, political realists urge us to start in the reality of politics and the context in which practices of political agency take place. Proper principles of political legitimacy should be theorised from *within* the actual workings of politics rather than from some abstract 'external' moral standpoint (Rossi and Sleat 2014; Bellamy 2010; Geuss 2008; Philp 2010).

Furthermore, critics share the methodological stance that governing principles are dependent on the practice under scrutiny in the sense that the practice puts substantial limitations on the appropriate normative principles for regulating it, for example by conditioning the principles, or making them meet certain criteria of 'fitness' (Valentini 2011: 404, 409; Jubb 2016: 78–9; Banai et al. 2011: 49–55; Rossi and Sleat 2014: 696; Mills 2005). In other words, we cannot justify an appropriate normative principle without first understanding the practice (in particular its point and purpose) upon which this principle is supposed to apply. And reaching such an understanding requires that the theorist engages in thoroughgoing interpretation (Valentini 2011: 404; Sangiovanni 2008; Mills 2005). It is argued that this methodological stance is superior to the methodologies adopted by mainstream political theory for identifying and justifying normative political principles such as those of justice or political legitimacy (Mills 2005: 172; Jubb 2016; Banai et al. 2011; Rossi and Sleat 2014).

Indeed, critics in these debates have different aims (theorising justice, legitimacy and so on) and hold on to these methodological commitments for different reasons (epistemic, normative, practical purchase and so on), and so we do not mean to suggest that they share a single, comprehensive method in a full-fledged sense. Rather, their shared methodological commitments may be summarised in terms of two core premises, which are incorporated into otherwise different accounts. First, they involve a meta-norm stating that the content and justification of a normative political principle is dependent on the practice it is supposed to govern. Second, they involve a practice-focused interpretive methodology for deriving these principles from facts about the practice in question (Erman and Möller 2015c: 534). This interpretive approach is fleshed out in different ways, but as we saw in Chapter 2, it typically consists of three main steps. First, the theorist tries to reach an understanding of the point and purpose of the practice in question, after which she seeks out the best interpretation of what role a normative political principle is envisioned to play applied to this practice in a second step. This then serves as the input for the third step, in which the theorist investigates what specific principle best regulates the practice. For many users of this interpretive approach, especially in the justice debate, an important source of inspiration is Ronald Dworkin's constructive interpretation (Dworkin 1986, Ch. 2), according to which an interpretation of the aim and purpose of the practice that a principle is supposed to govern – from the standpoint of the participants – is seen as a central piece of input for the normative second step of the method.[1]

As we mentioned in Chapter 2, we refer to these two premises as the 'practice-based method'. Below we investigate how this method may be understood and motivated as well as analyse what problems it faces in claiming to put certain limitations on normative political principles. According to its advocates, what differentiates the method from mainstream methods in political theory is not any particular set of value premises, but the *methodology* as such (Jubb 2016; Banai et al. 2011). The next two sections examine different understandings of the practice-based method in the literature and how it is said to condition normative principles.

THE PRACTICE-BASED METHOD AS AN OPEN METHOD

Whether the practice-based method puts limitations on normative political principles depends on what restrictions it comes with. On one plausible reading, the method is non-restrictive in the sense that it stresses the importance of starting with existing practices and points to the advantages of doing so, but makes no claim of this being the *exclusive* method for justifying normative principles. The method may thus be complemented with other ways of finding relevant facts and plausible candidates for principles and norms. This 'open interpretation' of the practice-based method is adopted by many theorists in the debate on ideal and non-ideal theory (Valentini 2012; Beitz 2009; Estlund 2011; Nagel 2005; Arvan 2014; Swift 2008; Stemplowska 2008).

The open interpretation of the method is intuitively attractive, but it introduces a challenge for theorists who insist that the method comes with particular constraints on normative political principles that would be rejected by mainstream theorists (Sangiovanni 2008; Jubb 2016; Banai et al. 2011; Rossi and Sleat 2014; Mills 2005). The challenge comes in the familiar form of the method of *reflective equilibrium* (Rawls 1951, 1971).[2] On reflective equilibrium, the theorist brings up all of her relevant beliefs for normative scrutiny, pondering on her basic normative intuitions ('considered judgements') about specific cases as well as the general principles she (initially) believes in. Based on these beliefs, and by searching for new information and arguments to bring into the equation (in order to avoid reaching a narrow equilibrium only), the theorist aims to reach a point where the beliefs are revised to be in equilibrium, coherently fitting together. Most probably, this means that she has to abandon some of her specific normative intuitions. Importantly, however, this is true of her principles too: if she finds that on closer examination they go against normative intuitions that she is simply not prepared to forsake, the principles must be revised (Erman and Möller 2015c: 535).

Reflective equilibrium is not only widely accepted in political theory – it is endorsed by presumed opponents of the practice-based method, too. Caney, for example, works explicitly with this method in theorising justice (Caney 2005). Even Cohen stresses that his account need not deny the process of reflective equilibrium (Cohen 2003: 224, n. 14). In other words, mainstream theorists may well endorse a methodological emphasis on existing practices and institutions in order to clarify the implicit commitments we hold – in matters of fact and value alike – so that we may better develop and justify principles of justice for a society or an institutional system (local or global). But, again, this does not preclude them from striving for or utilising more general principles of justice, principles that are compatible (otherwise something has to go) with more contextual ones but go beyond them in applicability.

In a nutshell, the problem posed by reflective equilibrium is the following: since reflective equilibrium tells us to bring up *all* potentially relevant considerations, it is completely neutral with regard to where we start our normative endeavour – we may start with abstract principles or with norms in ongoing local practices. The practice-based method is thus one of many possible approaches for investigating a normative issue fully in line with reflective equilibrium. Hence, on the open interpretation, the practice-based method does not come with any particular restrictions on principles at all.

Let us consider a possible retreat position for the practice-based theorist, taking the form of an accusation of neglect. The charge would be that while mainstream theorists accept that looking closely at actual practices and carefully investigating their workings in detail is a viable option in theorising normative political principles, they de facto never do. Since practice-based theorists actually do pursue such investigations, their theories are better (more justified). In order to defend this claim, however, practice-based theorists would have to offer a principled argument for why practices play a more important role than mainstream accounts have allowed for. But this path has not been explored in the literature. Rather, practice-based theorists usually insist that there is more to the practice-based method than merely stressing a practical neglect of mainstream theory. Let us therefore move to the stronger claims made about the method (Erman and Möller 2015c: 536).

THE PRACTICE-BASED METHOD AS A DISTINCT METHOD

Typically, practice-based theorists contend that there is more to the practice-based method than the open interpretation allows for. There have mainly been two strategies employed in the literature – which we call here the 'exclusivity strategy' and the 'interpretative strategy', respectively – to support the claim that the practice-based method is *theoretically* distinct from mainstream political theory and comes with a number of restrictions on normative political principles.[3]

The Exclusivity Strategy

The exclusivity strategy holds that *only* by looking at the actual practice we intend to regulate and by interpreting the relevant facts of this practice can we properly justify its normative political principles. 'Top-down' elements such as utilising abstract or idealised hypothetical cases or suggested general principles are considered unsuitable. Such a strong interpretation of the practice-based method indeed comes with heavy restrictions on normative political principles.

One version of this strategy is defended by Charles Mills in the debate on ideal and non-ideal theory. Mills argues that accounts which utilise concepts and principles that are not based in the actual socio-political context but belong to an ideal sphere (of justice or the like) are fundamentally flawed to the extent of being dangerous (Mills 2005: 173–5; see also Galston 2010). In his view, the abstract and higher-level principles defended by ideal theorists ignore present injustices and lose the conceptual tools to capture what ought to be done. Ideal theory is ideological in the sense that it consists of values and ideas that reflect the interests and experiences of a small group of white middle-to-upper-class males, which are mistakenly taken to be representative of other persons and groups in society (Mills 2005: 167–8, 172). For example, such an ideal will abstract away relations of structural domination and coercion, as well as visualise human agents in unrealistic ways through idealised institutions and capacities, neglecting how actual institutions and agents function (Mills 2005: 168–9; cf. Erman and Möller 2013: 25).

Instead of using idealised concepts such as 'autonomy' or 'justice', which allegedly distort our view by ignoring actual injustices, Mills' alternative approach makes use of what he calls 'non-idealised concepts', such as 'class society','patriarchy'and 'sexual harassment', which in his view help us to formulate truly liberating principles, rather than unattainable idealisations (Mills 2005: 172). For example, when using the term 'patriarchy', we force people to condemn certain oppressive practices without idealisations. Non-idealised concepts thus function as what Mills calls 'visual aids', since they help us to see what is wrong in the world as well as realise what we should do about it. Since such concepts capture a perspective of subordination which 'crystallize[s] in part from experience rather than being a priori', ideal theories that ignore these realities are necessarily 'handicapped in principle', according to Mills (2005: 176–7).

The challenge for this type of argument is twofold. First, it is unclear whether a distinction between idealised (bad) and non-idealised (good) concepts can be upheld. Let us accept for the sake of argument the unorthodox talk of a concept being non-idealised when it can be used to describe an actual state of the world, and idealised when it cannot. If so,'patriarchy','sexual harassment'and 'class society' are indeed non-idealised concepts. But so are those concepts Mills takes to be idealised. Let us compare 'gender inequality' with 'gender equality'. On Mills' account, the former is non-idealised (describes the world) while the latter is supposedly idealised. But surely this cannot be right. To begin with, we can always use negations and correctly describe the world with a claim such as: 'We do not have gender equality in any society in the world.' While this is of course trivially true, it immediately calls into question why idealised concepts could not be visual aids, to use Mills' words. Second, and more importantly, even though we don't have gender equality in any society at large, there are arguably relationships, workplaces and so on that are gender equal. Hence, the concept of gender equality can also be correctly used to describe the world in positive terms ('Anne and Ben have a gender equal relationship') just as well as it can be used to make false claims ('Most relationships are gender equal').[4] In other words, the sought-after states that ideal theory typically aims for, such as states of equality or non-domination, are not mere 'fantasy states' as claimed by Mills; they are obtained, if only on a more local scale.

In addition, even if the distinction could be upheld, it remains to be explained why idealised concepts distort rather than *complement* the perspective we gain from utilising the many non-idealised concepts we typically trade in. The concept of *vision zero* in traffic safety is idealised in the sense that each and every year some people *do* die in traffic. Still it seems to describe a desirable state of affairs, and it seems highly implausible (or at least unsupported) that the reality of traffic safety is distorted for policy-makers or theorists by formulating this ideal goal (Erman and Möller 2015c: 537).

The upshot of this is not merely that higher-order principles offered by mainstream theorists can comprise concepts that can be applied to actual practices of the real world, for example by demonstrating how an ideal state of affairs (for example, global equality) can be 'extrapolations' of more limited actual states (for example, local equality); it also calls into question to what extent normative political principles *should* be dependent on such contingent conditions at all. For example, suppose that no present heterosexual relationship was gender equal. Why would a principle that demands that a just society should be gender equal then be flawed, if it should be freed from the accusation of idealisation were there but one such relationship? It is not whether, or to what degree, a concept is realised by an actual property of the world that is important for a theory of justice, but whether the concept, as it is used, does in fact give us important visual aids. And this may be – and often is – the case even when the property as such is not instantiated in the present world.

The Interpretive Strategy

A second, quite different strategy for arguing in favour of the practice-based method has been the interpretive strategy, which refers to the idea of a conceptual difference between *interpretation* and *application* to chisel out a distinct method entailing certain constraints on normative political principles. On this view, 'starting in the actual' means to formulate a principle by interpreting the aims of a practice, and this interpretation is different from the traditional practice-independent methodology of simply applying a principle to this practice (Jubb 2016; Sangiovanni 2008; Banai et al. 2011). Andrea Sangiovanni uses an example from traffic safety to demonstrate the difference. For the mainstream theorist, Sangiovanni contends, there are only grounding moral principles and values, 'principles that can be directly derived from [them] and different contextual applications' (2008: 147). Thus, there is only a general principle such as 'drive only as fast as road conditions allow' and contextual information such as 'the road is wet', which leads to the more specific principle, 'drive at 20 mph'. By contrast, for the theorist using the practice-based method the contextual facts are instead part of what 'shapes the reasons we might have for endorsing specific principles . . . rather than the courses of action we should adopt in implementing them' (Sangiovanni 2008: 147).

In this example, the fact (among others) that constitutes a reason for an interpretative, contextual principle seems to be that the road is wet. However, on closer examination, this seems to be the very same fact that is doing (part of) the shaping of the principle of the mainstream theorist in formulating the principle 'drive at 20 mph'. So, it seems to be the case that the 'application story' can be retold in terms of an 'interpretation story', such that it merely becomes two ways of saying the same thing.

Practice-based theorists have tried to respond to this challenge by spelling out the distinction between application and interpretation in terms of the *dynamic* properties of the interpretative strategy versus the *static* properties of the mainstream account. Here the mainstream method for formulating principles for a specific practice is taken to consist of utilising an independently justified principle, such as a principle of equality, and then trying to grasp which applied principle this given premise would result in (Sleat 2016: 33; Geuss 2008: 8; Jubb 2016: 82). This approach is then contrasted with the practice-based method, according to which no pre-given principles are taken into account: all principles are developed from the demands of the situation, that is, *from interpretations of the facts of the case at hand alone* (Jubb and Rossi 2015; Jubb 2016: 82). The mainstream method is thus depicted as a static, one-tool-for-all-tasks approach, whereas the practice-based method is seen as dynamic, and better suited to accommodate the unique demands of a specific practice.

However, this interpretation seems to fly in the face of the previous remarks on reflective equilibrium being the method that most political theorists endorse. If the dialectical situation were between one theorist already committed to practice-independent principles and another completely non-committed, the latter would arguably have a more dynamic or flexible approach. But this conflates the *initial* commitments of a theorist with the *outcome* of the reflective/deliberative process (the post-interpretative step). Post-interpretively, the mainstream theorist is, *ex hypothesis*, committed to a general principle that she applies to the practice at hand, whereas the theorist using the practice-based method is not. But this says nothing about the dynamics of the deliberative process.[5] According to reflective equilibrium, no principle has the status of a premise that we cannot question; any particular commitment we have when entering the reflective deliberation may be questioned. Moreover, as will be further discussed in the next section, defenders of the practice-based method must face the objection that they, *pace* their emphasis on contextual facts shaping reasons, bring just as many initial principles and values into the deliberation as the mainstream theorist. *All* processes of normative evaluation start out with values and principles (however provisionally and unclearly formulated) to which the theorist commits (Erman and Möller 2015c: 538, 2016a: 15).

But let us consider the potential objection that it is not mainstream theorists who reject reflective equilibrium (by holding on to fixed higher-order principles), but theorists adopting the practice-based method, and *therefore* their methodological considerations entail constraints on normative political principles. The argument would go something like this: while in reflective equilibrium there are no a priori fixed points, there is on closer inspection such a fixed point for supporters of the practice-based method, namely the point and purpose of the practice to which a principle is supposed to apply. That this fixed point delimits the potential principles would thus be something that our analysis so far has failed to acknowledge.

Admittedly, in isolation some formulations of practice-dependent theorists, non-ideal theorists and political realists do lend themselves to this interpretation. But if we look more closely at how they in fact go about justifying normative political principles, the practice in question constitutes no such a priori fixed point. Indeed, to understand the point and purpose of the practice is regarded as central, and there seems to be a normative conviction that the principle should fit this purpose. But every supporter of the practice-based method will have normative convictions that she is less willing to give up when striving towards a state of coherence. Sometimes it is clear that the points and purposes of practices are simply too indefensible to hold on to. For example, while political realists argue that principles of political legitimacy are supposed to secure stability and social order (Williams 2005: 3), 'a peaceful situation preserved entirely through suppression or tyranny' cannot be legitimate (Horton 2010: 439). Likewise, practices where one group exercises unmediated coercion over another must be rejected, according to practice-dependent theorists, since they have no foothold upon which a conception of justice can be constructed (Sangiovanni 2008: 163). In their view, whatever principle best regulates a specific practice, it must be consistent with a moral principle of some kind (Banai et al. 2011; Ronzoni 2011; Sangiovanni 2008; James 2012). So if the aim of a practice were to abolish this principle, there is something wrong with the practice and it should *not* be a fixed point in our theorising about appropriate principles of justice.

METHODS OF JUSTIFICATION

We have so far looked at different understandings of the practice-based method and argued that in none of its plausible forms is it warranted to claim that it entails specific constraints on normative political principles. Of course, it is always possible to show how practices due to method-ological considerations condition normative principles if we defend a reading of the practice-based method utilising objectionable normative sources. This raises the question of what methods of justification are employed by practice-based theorists. According to them, as we have seen, it is only through careful interpretation of social and political practices that we get an adequate understanding of 'the real structures of oppression and exclusion that characterize the social and political order' needed to justify appropriate normative principles (Mills 2005: 181). The question that immediately arises is through what method of justification are these oppressive practices discovered and interpreted as oppressive rather than as something else? As practice-based theorists are well aware, we cannot extract *every* component of a normative principle from facts about the practice it is supposed to regulate, since in order for an account to be normative rather than merely descriptive, it must always in principle be possible for a person, group or community to be wrong about what should be done. Hence, not all sources of normativity utilised to theorise normative principles are entirely *internal* to the practice that the principles are intended to govern. Some are *external* in the sense that they are not necessarily extracted from the ideas, actions and beliefs of the participants. But where does this external normative source come from if it is not part of the practice in question, and how is it justified? Theorists adopting the practice-based method have tried to respond to these concerns.[6] Below we analyse the two main responses in current debates and discuss the problems they encounter.

One method of justification has been to utilise the idea of overlapping practices.[7] Instead of apprehending practices as more or less isolated phenomena, practice-based theorists stress that we live in a world of overlapping and mutually interdependent practices, in which '[the] rules of each practice often have a major impact on the internal functioning of other practices' (Banai et al. 2011: 56; Ronzoni 2009; Jubb 2016). For this reason, we are not confined to one isolated practice when theorising the best principles for regulating it. Rather, principles justified via the practice-based method have 'the potential of serving emancipatory goals' because they may well demand that practices are abolished which 'stand in contradiction to other practices of greater normative significance' (Banai et al. 2011: 56). Importantly, though, this is done 'for *practice-dependent reasons*' derived from the global web of overlapping practices (Banai et al. 2011: 57; Ronzoni 2009; Jubb 2016).

But how do overlapping practices get this emancipatory force? If the force does not come from external moral principles transcending the beliefs of the participants (which will be treated next), the normative potential seems to come from the added principles and values endorsed by the participants of these practices. Consider, for example, a group of people taking part in an oppressive practice which overlaps with a human rights practice justified by the participants through some moral principle. In such a case, the practice-based method could be used to point at incoherence and tensions between the practices to argue that practices demand the abolition of their own or other practices (Ronzoni 2009: 231; Jubb 2016).

We see at least two problems with this idea. First, given the current assumption about no transcending moral principles, it is not easy to see what means we have at our disposal to settle such tensions one way or the other, that is, deciding which practice has 'greater normative significance'; in this case, deciding whether oppression is more significant than human rights. Second, even if we assume, with practice-based theorists, that incoherence and tension is sufficient to demand the abolition of oppressive practices from the standpoint of justice (Ronzoni 2009: 231; see also Jubb 2016), the method seems very weak, leaving us with nothing to say in situations that strike us as clear cases of injustice. For according to this line of reasoning, as long as practices such as slavery (oppressive to most of us) are sufficiently coherent and do not happen to overlap with, for example, a human rights practice, no principles of justice could be formulated and justified. For that particular practice, justice is out of reach, as it were. Of course, this may be an intelligible position. But to say that justice is not applicable to the most despicably oppressive societies just because their practices happen to be coherent seems to be a high price to pay for fidelity to the practice-based method. While it would indeed make the method distinct from mainstream approaches and entail that practices heavily constrain normative political principles, we cannot see why it would be attractive or even defensible (Erman and Möller 2015c: 541–2).

A second method of justification among practice-based theorists has been to tie the practice-based method to a moral or political value or principle of some kind. For example, practice-dependent theorists argue that whatever principle best regulates a specific practice, it must be consistent with a moral principle of some kind, such as the principle of equal moral worth (Banai et al. 2011; Ronzoni 2011; Sangiovanni 2007, 2008) or the principle of reasonable non-rejectability (James 2012). However, this moral principle is not regarded as a principle of justice proper, but merely a moral requirement that every conception of justice has to include. It is then the task of the theorist adopting the practice-based method to work out what it means for a specific practice to respect this moral requirement. Importantly, though, it is emphasised that the practice-based approach is 'not itself a moral position' but only a *methodology* (Banai et al. 2011: 50).

Since the normative source cannot be derived from the concept of justice as such, here the idea must be that this moral principle is intended as a practice-*independent* constraint on the method or the principles generated by it. As argued by both James and Sangiovanni, it is a moral criterion that is not extracted from any particular practice (James 2012: 29). Rather, it indicates when a practice *meets* a moral standard (James 2005: 311–12). A principle of justice, on the other hand, is internal relative to a practice in the sense that it would not apply in the absence of this practice (James 2012; Sangiovanni 2008, 2011).

However, with such practice-independent constraints tied to the method, the suspicion reappears that the methodology used by mainstream political theorists is in fact the same after all and hence that no additional constraints on normative political principles follow from being committed to the practice-based method (Christensen 2013). In light of our previous discussion, with both methods endorsing general moral principles external to the practices under scrutiny as well as the influence of the actual workings of these practices for the content of the governing normative principle, it becomes a difficult task for proponents of the practice-based method to chisel out a significant *theoretical* difference between the two camps. As the analysis above reveals, maintaining that there is a sense in which a principle of justice becomes 'internal relative to a practice' only with the practice-based method gets little traction until a distinction such as that between interpretation and application has been corroborated. Not until then is it viable to argue that only with the practice-based method is the governing principle for a practice perceived as a principle of, say, justice, rather than an *application* of a general principle of justice – or a 'rule of regulation' in Cohen's terminology (2003: 242). Since this distinction must be more than merely terminological, the label of the governing principle cannot play a substantial role (Erman and Möller 2015c: 542).

In addition, defenders of the practice-based method seem to put themselves in a philosophically perplexing place, for why would some normative principles – in this case normative *political* principles such as principles of justice – be practice-dependent whereas other, say, higher-level moral principles would not? It is difficult to see on what grounds practice-based theorists could make this distinction. Yet, when it is argued that practice-based theorists can 'always point to basic moral failures that need no real interpretation to condemn', such a distinction is precisely what seems to be implied, suggesting that principles of justice are dependent on the interpretation of practices while other normative principles are not (Jubb 2016: 86).

To sum up, in this chapter we have analysed a recent method-ological turn in political theory, in which the practice-based method has taken a central place in several debates. We have reviewed and evaluated various readings of this method and have shown the many problems that the stronger 'distinct' reading face. Importantly, though, these theoretical problems must not be conflated with *first-order* con-tributions made by theorists adopting the practice-based method. We must carefully distinguish between demonstrating the superiority of a method as such and making a normative contribution in political theory by using that method. Miriam Ronzoni's analysis of Cohen's socialist principles is a case in point. This is a nice example of how careful interpretation of the point and purpose of different societal practices may bring to light problems in normative theorising. Cohen defends two principles – the egalitarian principle and the principle of community – by looking at the practice of a camping trip (Cohen 2009). What Ronzoni shows is that while the two principles may be appropriate for regulating a camping trip, the camping trip model is not suitable for regulating social practices that function very differ-ently, such as the family. In contrast to the camping trip, the purpose of a family is not monistic or discontinuous in time, and participants of this practice typically have much stronger emotional ties (Ronzoni 2011: 179–80). The analysis is a great illustration of how useful the practice-based method can be to expose how things may go wrong if we neglect the actual workings of the practice that, in this case, is used as metaphor for society at large (for example, how it deviates from other practices in society).

But a good normative argument utilising a method does not dem-onstrate its general advantages *qua* methodology in theorising norma-tive political principles. In our view, Ronzoni's analysis is an example of good old-fashioned first-order theorising, which exposes problems of using an analogy when theorising normative principles, urging us to be suspicious of Cohen's intuition pump. However, nothing in the analysis lends her ammunition to draw any conclusions about the prac-tice-based method as better at arriving at justified principles, which she elsewhere insists that it is (Ronzoni 2009; Banai et al. 2011). To prove such superiority, she would have to show not only that Cohen's prin-ciples applied to *society* are false, but also argue for a better theory of justice in a way that demonstrates the superiority of the practice-based method. And to do so requires that the theorist looks at society at large (Erman and Möller 2015c: 543).

In view of the many problems that the strong 'distinct' reading of the method faces, we conclude that the weaker 'open' reading is the only one plausible, but that this reading does not allow for the constraints on principles that its proponents imagine. According to the open interpretation, the practice-based method is seen as useful but no claims are made with regard to it being the exclusive method for justifying normative political principles.

NOTES

1. Together with the meta-norm, the interpretive method should thus produce principles that are sensitive to/dependent on the nature of the practice to which they are supposed to apply. However, this must not be misunderstood. Sensitivity to the nature of the practice does not simply mean that a regulative principle is formulated so that it satisfies a condition of applicability (more on this in Chapter 7). More demandingly, it means that principles are constrained by understandings implicit *in* the practice, such as its aims and purpose according to its participants, its public rules and norms, its history and so on.

2. Alternatively, reflective equilibrium may refer more narrowly to a state of coherence of a belief system rather than to a methodology (more on this in Chapter 7). In the main text, however, we follow the methodological interpretation more commonplace in current political theory.

3. It might look tempting for proponents of the practice-based method to utilise a *particularist* objection when arguing against mainstream accounts and in favour of the practice-based method. Particularists argue that morality or politics is essentially contextual, and are sceptical of the existence (or at least usefulness) of principles for guiding our conduct (cf. Hooker and Little 2000). If particularists are right, we should indeed study only the actual context. As we discussed in Chapter 2, however, the particularist objection is not raised by practice-based theorists, and for a good reason: since the very existence/usefulness of principles are denied on particularism, not only abstract but *all* principles must be eschewed. Supporters of the practice-based method, although critical of mainstream uses (and formulations) of principles, are firm believers in them. Consequently, particularism would be self-defeating for the theorist using the practice-based method.

4. Or, more precisely, the term 'gender equality' expressing the concept of gender equality can be used. For simplicity, we will in the main text talk of 'applying' and 'using' concepts even when, technically, linguistic items are applied or used.

5. In fact, practice-dependent theorists have been criticised for having an overly linear and non-dynamic view of the different stages of the interpretive methodology (see Beitz's critique of James, Beitz 2014: 233).
6. See Charles Beitz (2014) for an instructive analysis of different uses of the distinction of internal/external to practice at work in James (2012).
7. Note here that we accept for the sake of argument that it is possible to individuate a social practice such that its boundaries are drawn in an uncontroversial way (which is the aim of the so-called 'pre-interpretive' stage). To do so, however, seems tremendously difficult. We agree with Beitz that in contrast to the legal interpretation of statutes – which was the object of interpretation that Dworkin had in mind for his interpretive methodology – there may be no uncontroversial way of delimiting a social practice (Beitz 2014: 231–3; see also Julius 2014: 244–5).

Chapter 5

EPISTEMOLOGICAL CONSTRAINTS

If the methodological aspects of how to best understand the relationship between social and political practices and normative political principles have received a lot of attention in current debates, much less attention has been directed at epistemological aspects. Yet, during the last few years, we have witnessed an increased attempt to utilise a set of *epistemic* premises in order to justify constraints in political theory. In this chapter, we will discuss three such epistemological constraints which, while originating from substantially different debates, evoke interestingly similar justificatory strategies: according to its proponents, the epistemic premises pointed to not only supply *contributing* reasons for the constraints sought, but also entail a *rational requirement* to accept the constraints given the truth of the premises.

The first two epistemological constraints treated in the chapter originate from the practice-dependence debate. They both focus on alleged deficiencies in our first-order knowledge in the political domain. The first constraint relates to what we call 'descriptive uncertainty': we have, according to practice-dependent theorists, insufficient or too uncertain knowledge about central empirical circumstances of politics, and therefore a practice-dependent approach is required (and, implicitly, the statist or at least non-cosmopolitan conclusions they infer from using this approach). The second constraint relates to what we call 'value uncertainty', which refers to a state where we are uncertain about which values or principles we endorse. In such cases, it has recently been argued that a certain form of practice-dependent methodology (so-called 'mediated deduction') is required.

The proponents of the arguments of descriptive and value uncertainty further claim that, at least in most cases, these constraints hold in the world as we know it. Consequently, the arguments are allegedly not only valid (true given the premises) but also sound: based on true premises, the practice-dependent methodology is required in the political reality in which we find ourselves.

The third epistemological constraint is utilised by theorists referred to in Chapter 2 as 'pragmatist epistemic theorists', such as Cheryl Misak and Robert Talisse, who claim that a certain set of fundamental epistemic premises are sufficient for justifying democracy. More specifically, they argue that mainstream political theory (e.g. Rawls and Dworkin) has failed to offer a plausible justification of democracy since it relies on a justification in terms of moral values and principles that are liberal but not universally shared. A more promising path, according to pragmatist epistemic theorists, is to justify democracy on epistemic grounds. On this view, all of us are committed to a set of fundamental epistemic meta-principles, on pain of being irrational. So, despite moral disagreement, we are rationally required to endorse a rather demanding model of democracy, namely, deliberative democracy.

In the chapter, we demonstrate that all three argumentative strategies fail even when we assume the truth of their respective premises. That is, although we find the support for several of the epistemic premises unconvincing, we will in this chapter (for the most part) assume their truth and argue that the conclusions sought are not justified.

DESCRIPTIVE UNCERTAINTY

'Descriptive uncertainty', as we use the expression, concerns uncertainty about the empirical facts. More precisely, here we refer to arguments for practice-dependence that use as the grounding premise a state of insufficient, unclear or uncertain empirical knowledge. Recently, several theorists have defended a practice-dependent approach in light of descriptive uncertainty. In what follows, we will focus primarily on Aaron James, who has argued for a practice-dependent account of fair trade partly by utilising an argument from epistemic uncertainty (James 2012), as well as Ayelet Banai, Miriam Ronzoni and Christian Schemmel's recent argument for a practice-dependent approach to justice (Banai et al. 2011), also through a premise of descriptive uncertainty.

In his account of fair trade, James builds on his earlier work on practice-dependence, which he now applies to one particular domain: the global economy. James' general method is the three-step interpretive methodology of justification described in Chapters 2 and 4. In a first, pre-interpretive, step aiming to identify the relevant practice in uncontroversial, sociological terms, James concludes that the global economy is organised by a distinctive kind of international practice of trade, in which countries mutually rely on common markets (James 2012: 15–16). As the reader may recall, the aim of the second interpretive step is to offer an analysis of the practice in question in order to consider whether it can, in some form, ultimately be justified. Here James argues that the national income gains from trade are the result of international cooperation in the form of mutual market reliance, the practice whereby countries rely on goods and services for the sake of mutual economic gain (James 2012: 19). James argues that in this way the global economy generates distinctive egalitarian responsibilities 'independently of other moral or justice concerns which might equally apply in the global economy's absence' (James 2012: 17). In the third – post-interpretive – step, James makes an assessment of 'what structural organization is reasonably acceptable to each party affected, as framed by the underlying (perhaps moralized) conception of the practice' (James 2012: 28).

On James' analysis, the global economy is essentially embedded in government decisions on trade and currency policy, together with international arrangements for the coordination of those decisions. The state system is thus 'not only the primary regulator of economic interdependence but a constitutive condition of its very existence' (James 2012: 13). Therefore, if political philosophy is to be normative *for us*, James asserts, it must begin from our international political system 'simply for lack of a well-assured alternative for the management of global-sized affairs' (James 2012: 104). James defends three principles of fairness for trade ('principles of equity') – the principle of collective due care, the principle of international relative gains and the principle of domestic relative gains – and argues that these are practice-dependent in a dual sense: they are justified not only *for* the practice in question but also in part *'from* its implicit understandings' (James 2012: 29).

This account of fairness, James claims, is a mid-position between cosmopolitan and domestic egalitarian approaches, thus avoiding the former's fault of obscuring 'the distinctively international structure' of the fairness responsibilities emerging from the global economy, as well as the latter's fault of restricting the concerns for socioeconomic justice to the domestic domain (James 2012: 9–10). For our purposes, however, it is not the details of James' positive account that is of interest, but his argument for the claim that an account of just trade requires a practice-dependent approach. James argues that in order for a political account to apply to us, the recommended principles must address the available human means for resolving the moral problem of assurance, that is, the central coordination problem of being able to count on the behaviour of others. Principles of justice can only require arrangements that we can know with reasonable confidence that we can jointly establish and maintain (James 2012: 116). And for this to be the case, the approach has to be practice-dependent (James 2012: 104).

In James' view, the root of the problem is what we call descriptive uncertainty. For James, the requirement of availability is not logical or physical, relating to what is logically or physically available from where we stand, but explicitly epistemic (James 2012: 114–17). James' thought here is that a basic feature of the human condition is a lack of direct knowledge of (and control over) the minds of others, which in turn entails an uncertainty about what others will do. This basic risk involved in cooperation is a fundamental feature of nearly all human social interaction, even under the best of cooperative circumstances (James 2012: 58). Therefore, James argues, not even morally motivated agents within an ideal-theoretical framework can be expected to cooperate and act in agreement with others unless some expectations of regulation or patterns of coordination are established in a jointly available way (2012: 114–15). And since only a practice-dependent account may give us knowledge, 'with reasonable confidence', of whether a suggested principle of justice requires arrangements possible to establish and maintain given our current situation, only a practice-dependent method, with its in-depth interpretation of actual practices, respects the limitations which the demands of epistemic availability put on abstraction and idealisation (James 2012: 117).

Another example of descriptive uncertainty allegedly requiring a practice-dependent approach appears in the recent work of Banai et al. 2011. In their view, many principles of justice – paradigmatically cosmopolitan principles – are too abstract, and too detached from how practices and institutions function, to give us sufficient knowledge of the (empirical) states of the world the principles would require. Abstract principles of global justice 'cannot even be evaluated as to their very soundness, because the means necessary to do so are lacking' (Banai et al. 2011: 51). In other words, we lack sufficiently detailed knowledge of the required circumstances for the abstract principle to apply. Moreover, our knowledge of many of the potential alternatives is simply not available. The idea of a world state, for example, is too fictitious, too unspecified in the details, for us to know how the political arrangements in it would work in practice and, hence, whether it really is morally and politically acceptable.

Principles justified through a practice-dependent method, however, do not have this problem, Banai et al. argue, since such principles are properly based on the interpretation of actual practices (2011: 52). In such cases, there is sufficient descriptive information about the practices and institutions to assess the suggested principles that are supposed to apply.

While not uncontroversial, it seems to us that the premise of descriptive uncertainty alluded to by practice-dependent theorists does hold, at least to some extent. We do lack full knowledge about the behaviour of others or how the world would have to be for abstract or general principles to apply. Still, the practice-dependent conclusions do not follow, for at least two reasons.

First of all, that the premises hold *to some extent* does not mean that they hold in the strong sense assumed by the practice-dependent theorists. Reasonably, all levels of uncertainty do not require the same handling. If our uncertainty is extreme – so that we have no clue whatsoever about what others will do given a set of rules, or how the world would have to be in order for us to apply a given principle – other practical principles would apply, unless our uncertainty is limited. In James' argumentation, the evidentiary standard for judging that we have epistemic availability is that we have 'reasonable confidence', which supposedly reflects our 'reasonable uncertainty-aversion' (James 2012: 119). But while this standard may sometimes be rational, the argument neglects the diversity of evidentiary standards that may be justified, given different circumstances (Erman and Möller 2017b).

When testing new directions, we are often justified in accepting a less demanding standard. For example, we may often reasonably test new directions in a step-by-step manner even when lacking 'reasonable confidence'. Consider a principle of what we may call 'meta-assurance', which aims to respond to problems of assurance by offering ways to move from undesirable results while at the same time securing us from *irreversible* catastrophic developments. It seems reasonable that the evidentiary standard for meta-assurance is weaker than reasonable confidence and uncertainty-aversion, instead demanding something like 'reasonable uncertainty', allowing us to take risks insofar as we are secure against irrevocable results. A meta-assurance principle such as this seems to be a common approach in many areas. In much medical research, for example, especially in the early stages, experiments are carried out in a gradual and often fragmented fashion to develop new medicines. If such developments had been limited by James' strong demand of epistemic availability overall, many of the path-breaking discoveries that have led to the curing of pandemic diseases are unlikely to have taken place. Similarly, in actual politics different policy proposals are tested in this piecemeal fashion. Barring such possibilities seems to unduly limit the available options.

Second, and even more importantly, the argument for why we should accept the practice-dependent method as required fails even *granted* (1) that we accept the epistemic premise and (2) that we endorse the argument that the practice-dependent method gives us better knowledge of the empirical outcome of the principles justified by the method. Let us thus grant that lack of determinate knowledge of the behaviour of others, or knowledge of world-states given abstract principles, is a basic human condition. As we have stated above, this is far from clear, but seems sound given at least some interpretations. Let us further assume that practice-dependent theories have the advantage of providing us with better knowledge of how people would behave (cooperate in particular) and how the world would look like given the suggested principles. While, as far as we can see, there is nothing in the third step of the practice-dependent methodology as such that forces the theorist to avoid abstract or radical principles, the clear tendency of practice-dependent theorists has been to suggest principles that relatively closely correlate with those actually guiding the interpreted practices. Consequently, it seems reasonable to assume that they come close to minimising descriptive uncertainty.

Given these two assumptions, it seems sensible to acknowledge that the practice-dependent method fares better in relation to descriptive uncertainty than mainstream methods in political theory, which do not demand a similarly close attention to, or correspondence with, actual practices. But that a method is better in one respect neither establishes that it is better in all respects, nor that it is better overall. In other words, the conclusion that a method is required because it is better in one respect is fallacious. We may thus accept that epistemic availability is *one* value among many that we should consider when theorising what justice requires in different contexts, and even that it is an important one. But we still need a justification for why the suggested level of epistemic availability would be the only or even the most relevant aspect when evaluating a principle of justice. And such a justification is not provided in the existing arguments, nor do we see what such a justification would look like. Rather, it seems plausible that a theorist could resist the practice-dependent approach because she – on balance – prefers not to let, say, epistemic assurance considerations trump other central considerations, such as equality. All things considered, we may prioritise principles of cosmopolitan justice over James' principles of international justice *even if* they are less 'well assured'. Sometimes scenarios less clearly discernible in detail may be taken as normatively attractive, and an account of why this is mistaken is required for the epistemic motive to be sufficient for justifying the practice-dependent approach in light of descriptive uncertainty (Erman and Möller 2017b).

VALUE UNCERTAINTY

It is hardly surprising that practice-based theorists claim that their accounts have epistemic benefits since they pay special attention to actual practices, and therefore gain a more detailed and secure knowledge of the empirical circumstances in which their recommended principles are to function. Recently, however, an argument for the practice-dependent approach has been put forward by Andrea Sangiovanni based on the idea that it is required given a certain knowledge-deficiency regarding our normative commitments. When the content of our fundamental, higher-level principles is too vague or unclear to generate determinate prescriptions, Sangiovanni argues, a practice-dependent method he calls 'mediated deduction' is required in order to justify a normative political principle (Sangiovanni 2016).

Formally speaking, Sangiovanni's new claim is a retreat of sorts, in that the 'old' claim of practice-dependent theorists considered the practice-dependent method to be required for *all* justified theorising about politics (Sangiovanni 2008; Ronzoni 2009; Rossi 2012). In his later works, however, Sangiovanni acknowledges that for some principles, there is no need for a practice-dependent methodology. For the utilitarian, for example, a practice may be viewed as an instrument for realizing a set of higher-level principles and values for which we have independent justification. Our immediate practical aim is to reform (or transform) the rules and norms constitutive of the practice so as to better realise, on balance, those higher-level principles and values. (Sangiovanni 2016: 15)

This is so, Sangiovanni argues, since the higher-level principle, the principle of utility, which tells us to act so as to maximise the aggregated welfare of all persons, is sufficiently clear in its content for a direct, 'instrumental application' to be possible. We can, in other words, apply the principle of utility directly, expecting our practices and more applied principles to follow suit (Sangiovanni 2016: 15–17).

Often, however, the state of the independent higher-level principles we endorse is less clear-cut, and we need to develop intermediate principles to help us figure out and justify applied principles of justice. On this alternative 'mode of application', Sangiovanni explains,

we are less clear about the higher-level principles and values which apply; we are less clear, that is, about which higher-level principles and values we ought to use as standards for reform . . . To be sure, we have some idea about many higher-level principles and values . . . but, at this point in our reflection, they lack determinacy, or at any rate, enough determinacy to help us in our critical task. What we need, in short, are *mediating* principles – principles that bridge the gap between the higher-level principles and the lower-level norms and rules constitutive of the practice as it currently is. (Sangiovanni 2016: 15–16)

Sangiovanni points to a wide range of situations in which our normative commitments are uncertain in this way: situations in which we are unclear about which principles to endorse, their exact content and how they apply to the situation at hand. Since this knowledge deficit is related to values and norms, we will call it 'value uncertainty'.

Sangiovanni exemplifies the distinction between the instrumental and the mediated mode of application with the European Union (EU) as the entity for which we look for applied principles. The (instrumental) utilitarian, he envisions, may endorse a higher-level principle such as:

(U) We should select those applied principles that maximise the aggregate welfare of all persons.

Let us assume that EU-U is the principle (or set of principles) which, when applied to the EU, maximises the aggregated welfare of all persons. We have then, Sangiovanni argues, fully justified EU-U as the applied principle to regulate the EU (Sangiovanni 2016: 16).

Now, let us instead assume that we are committed to another higher-level principle, (M), whose application, as Sangiovanni sees it, lacks sufficient determinacy for direct application (Sangiovanni 2016: 17):

> (M) If one has engaged in long-standing, mutual and beneficial interaction, then one has an obligation to give a fair return to those involved.

Under the (reasonable) assumption that the EU gives rise to a long-standing mutual and beneficial interaction, the obligation to give a fair return is triggered. If it then turns out that the exact nature and structure of these interactions justify a certain principle, or set of principles, we have found a mediated principle for the EU. Let us call this principle (EU-M).[1]

On Sangiovanni's analysis, the instrumental and mediated modes illustrated above differ in a number of ways, and the justification of the applied principles – here EU-U and EU-M – works differently in a significant way for the two modes. Crucially, he argues that while EU-U may be directly justified through our reasons for believing (U), together with the empirical circumstances of the EU (more specifically: the evidence for what best maximises aggregated welfare), justification on the mediated deductive mode requires a more interpretative method:[2]

> Our justification ... requires an interpretation of the nature of, in this case, the EU. In the specific case of a principle of reciprocity, we need to know what kinds of mutually beneficial interaction the EU makes possible on the best interpretation of what the EU does. This general account of the EU's point and purpose, in turn, would give structure to our judgment that reciprocity, say, requires principles for different kinds of mutually beneficial interaction: one for relations among member states, and one for relations among EU citizens. (Sangiovanni 2016: 18–19)

In other words, while both modes require empirical investigations in order to justify their respective applied principles, mediated deduction comes with special demands. Sangiovanni concludes:

> I have argued that understanding the nature of a practice is crucial
> to the *justification* of a system of principles . . . This has an impor-
> tant methodological upshot: social interpretation of practices – in
> which we try to understand the point and purpose of a practice
> by seeking to characterise its underlying or motivating value or
> goodness (should it have any) – are central aspects of any political
> theory that aims to evaluate the existing practices from the point
> of view of higher-level values and principles [in circumstances of
> value uncertainty]. (Sangiovanni 2016: 20)

Hence, when the higher-level principles and values we endorse are
vague, not clearly specified or otherwise uncertain, we must engage in
a specific study of the nature of the practice in question. While, as we
stated initially, the scope of this claim is more limited than in previous
versions of the account, where the practice-dependent methodology
was required over the board, the scope is indeed still quite substantial. Arguably, the value uncertainty alluded to by Sangiovanni is the
typical case. Perhaps with the exception of utilitarianism,[3] most higher-
level principles seem lacking in specificity. From a deontological – or
indeed rights-based – perspective, the need for moral judgement in
the link between principle and application is often stressed (cf. Kant
1970; O'Neill 1987; Hooker 2000). Moreover, the uncertainty involved
in assessing the relative strength of different higher-level principles in
actual cases is well known. Thus, Sangiovanni's claim that mediated
deduction is required in such cases would have far-reaching consequences for political theory.

While it may be questioned whether Sangiovanni has managed to
mark out a theoretically important distinction by his account of instrumental and mediated 'modes of application',[4] the most pressing question in light of our purposes in this volume is whether there is any
merit in the claim that a certain interpretive method, which investigates
the nature of the practice in question, is needed in situations of value
uncertainty. This is what we turn to now.

INVESTIGATING THE NATURE OF THE PRACTICE

The term 'nature' may mean many things, and in order to evaluate Sangiovanni's thesis of the need to understand the nature of our practices
in circumstances of value uncertainty, we must get a clearer picture of

its intended use. This is not an easy task, since practice-dependent theorists are not always good at clearly defining their central terms. Fortunately, they have long stressed a number of significant aspects that help us to grasp their intended meanings. In particular, understanding the nature of the practice, for practice-dependent theorists, has both what we could call an 'objective' and a 'subjective' component, entailing knowledge of the practice as such as well as knowledge of how the participants of the practice view the nature of the practice and the salient values incorporated in it (Sangiovanni 2008: 140–55, 161; Sangiovanni 2016: 17–20; James 2012: 26–31, 186–95). In sum, understanding the nature of a practice entails:

1. knowledge of the point and purposes of the practice, the values explicitly or implicitly guiding the practice, and the structure of the interactions and relationships between participants of the practice (the objective component); and
2. knowledge of the underlying or motivating values and self-understandings of the participants of the practice, including their reasons for affirming the points and purposes of the practice (the subjective component).

Considering this dual understanding of the nature of the practice, it makes sense to stress, as Sangiovanni has done, that in order to justify an account of justice, we should aim to understand the role justice plays for the participants of the practice in question, and how the demands for justice enter within the historical and political context of the practice (Sangiovanni 2008: 150). Likewise, James has stressed how our moral concepts should 'answer to the canons of interpretation rather than of pure moral judgment' and how credible moral considerations should be regarded as 'presuppositions of moral concepts or conceptions that are explicitly recognized or implicitly assumed [in the practice]' (James 2012: 29).

It should now be reasonably clear that investigating the nature of a practice is a rather strong constraint, which sets a practice-dependent methodology apart from mainstream accounts where no such demand is made. But is it justified? In order for us to get an initial grip on the constraint, let us look at a somewhat more limited domain than the EU, namely the practice of penal institutions. Let us assume that in the prison context under investigation, the majority of the participants in the practice understand its point and purpose as rehabilitation in the sense of, say, minimising the (future) criminal population. The participants hold, we may further assume, a number of deontological values such that killing, stealing or being dishonest is intrinsically bad. What methodology, we may then ask, should navigate us in the prison context given this contextual setting?

Let us now consider two potential accounts, each aiming to justify a guiding principle for the penal system in the above context. On the first account, the theorist is a card-carrying utilitarian, endorsing a higher-level principle according to which we aim to maximise the welfare of people. On the second account, the theorist is a fairness retributionist for whom a fair distribution of burdens and benefits is essential and unfair advantages are morally problematic.[5]

In order to evaluate the investigative need in either of these two accounts, let us first clarify a point which has been rather quickly glossed over until now, namely the 'theory-neutral' need for empirical investigation. In order for any applied normative account to be justified, some set of empirical information is obviously needed. If we do not have any idea of how the practice functions, we would not have a clue whether the applied principle would help to maximise welfare or respect fairness. Practice-dependent theorists clearly acknowledge this. In several of his papers, Sangiovanni stresses that all theorists in the debate, practice-dependent or not, acknowledge the need for such contextual information. It is thus uncontroversial 'that information about existing institutional and political contexts is needed in coming to a concrete judgment regarding which particular course of action, regulatory rule, or policy is the best possible way forward from where we are now' (Sangiovanni 2016: 3). The controversial question is whether there is a more demanding informational need.

In the first case of the utilitarian, as we noted above, Sangiovanni argues that the uncontroversial contextual information is all that we need. The theorist does not need to investigate the nature of the practice of penal institutions in the demanding sense explicated above (we will implicitly assume this interpretation of 'nature' from now on); she merely needs to gain a sufficiently detailed idea of what penal principles will maximise the welfare of people, given the context at hand. And indeed, we agree with Sangiovanni here. For the utilitarian, all that ultimately matters is what leads to the best consequences. Hence, that the institutional point of prisons, from the perspective of the participants (or any other perspective, for that matter), is to mini-mise the criminal population is irrelevant as such to the utilitarian. This institutional point is only a good thing if it de facto maximises welfare. If other arrangements – such as house arrest, ankle monitor-ing or therapy – leads to more welfare, the principles for penal insti-tutions should directly reflect this, regardless of whether it minimises the criminal population.[6]

In the second case of the fairness retributionist, gaining unfair advantages over others is morally problematic in light of her funda-mental, higher-level principle. Let us now (reasonably) assume that the concept of fairness she uses is somewhat vague and undetermined. What exactly constitutes fairness – and absence thereof – is not given in detail by the higher-level principle, but must be worked out when applying the principle. Consequently, her account is in the state of value uncertainty which, according to Sangiovanni, requires knowledge of the nature of the practice. As far as we can tell, however, the fairness retributionist has no more obligations to perform such an investigation than does the utilitarian.

The main reason for this is that, just as in the case of the utilitarian, and also without investigating the nature of the practice, the fairness retributionist has the two components she needs for developing a justi-fied applied account: a guiding principle and contextual information. While she does not have a determined account of what constitutes fair-ness in every situation, her higher-level principle already tells her that fairness considerations are what ultimately matter. So while we have assumed that the participants in the practice take the point and purpose of penal institutions to be rehabilitation, and subscribe to a number of deontological values, since the fairness retributionist is already commit-ted to a particular view of what matters, she may reasonably infer that these sociological facts have no justificatory force at all. If these are the salient reasons for the people building and managing prisons, she may argue, they came about and are upheld for the wrong reasons.[7] Instead, the merit of penal practice is determined by fairness considerations: the justification of penal practices such as incarceration and education of criminal offenders depends on how they would infringe on fairness. In order to answer *that* question, we naturally need to know a lot of details of how penal practices function and what wider consequences they have for prisoners, their families and the society at large; but that, again, is 'merely' the sort of contextual information that all sides in the debate agree is needed for an applied principle (Erman and Möller 2017a, forthcoming).

Rather than being a function of how uncertain or undetermined our principles are, whether we are required to investigate the nature of a practice to develop an applied principle for regulating it seems to depend on the *content* of the higher-level principle, that is, what considerations are salient according to it. If the principle, for example, explicitly states that it is the motivating reasons and values of the participants of the practice that decide which values should guide it, we are of course required to investigate the practice when developing an applied principle. If our endorsed higher-level principle has a democratic content, in the sense of stating that the will of the participants should decide how the practice should be governed, investigating the values and motivations of the participants is perhaps required.[8] However, the level of vagueness or lack of clarity of the democratic higher-level principle as such does not matter; only that it tells us to investigate the preferences of the participants. For other higher-level principles – such as principles of utility, fairness or natural rights (or any number of suggested alternatives) – it may be reasonably argued that regardless of how fully specified they are, the point and purpose of the practice or the motivating reasons and values among the participants are irrelevant to the justification of the applied principles, as long as we have sufficient contextual information of the case at hand.

In other words, while there might be different interpretive problems involved in the two cases, corresponding to the distinct problems of figuring out what constitutes welfare as opposed to fairness, neither of them seems to require investigation of the nature of the practice as such. Indeed, this conclusion is fully in line with the classic idea of moral justification, where so-called 'headcount' approaches are deemed problematic: what people *think* to be morally right is different from what *is* morally right, since we may all in principle be wrong about a moral belief, just as in the case of natural beliefs (such as believing that the earth is flat). Likewise, a practice as a whole may be indefensible even when it is endorsed by all practitioners in it. Slavery is a good example of a practice which was thought to be legitimate by many practitioners, but which is no less illegitimate, and would be so even if even the slaves suffered from self-deception.

A potential objection to our argument so far may be that the constraint that Sangiovanni attempts to establish through an epistemic premise of value uncertainty should be given a weaker interpretation. After all, Sangiovanni sees his position in some sense as a retreat from the overly strong claims about the domain of the practice-dependent methodology of early versions of the approach. Thus, while practice-dependent theorists (including Sangiovanni) have stressed both objective and subjective aspects of 'understanding the nature of a practice', perhaps Sangiovanni is intending a retreat not only with regard to domain (i.e. when the method is applicable) but also with regard to the content of the methodology. Perhaps it is the case that only the objective aspect of understanding the nature of a practice, its actual point and purpose and its guiding values, is required, while understanding the subjective beliefs of the participants is optional.

Indeed, this weaker thesis seems to avoid many of the 'headcount' problems of the stronger claim. Still, the first of the two conditions of 'understanding the nature of the practice' also seems optional. First, the alleged criterion for when the practice-dependent method (mediated deduction) is required remains puzzling. Why would we need to investigate the point and purpose of the practice and the values underlying it in cases of value uncertainty but not otherwise? What are we supposed to learn, normatively speaking, from such an investigation that the 'usual', uncontroversial empirical investigation of the context of the practice has not already given us? Sangiovanni assumes it is the lack of specificity of the higher-level principle that necessitates such an investigation, but he gives us no reasons why, and we cannot find any support for the assumption in the writings of practice-dependent theorists (Erman and Möller 2017a).

Second, we find no support for the weaker claim that we need to investigate the nature of a practice (in the objective sense) over and above the contextual information that all sides of the debate acknowledge. To demonstrate this, let us start by looking at a practice where it does not seem too far-fetched to claim that it has a given point and purpose: the practice of (association) football. The point and purpose of football, let us assume (for the sake of argument), is to win while following the set of rules in the football rulebook. Now, our aim to justify an account of fair play in football is based on the higher-level principle that acting fair in sports requires that we never are deceitful. The principle in question lacks determinacy in the sense sought, since what deceitfulness amounts to is not further specified, but must be worked out when applying the principle to the case at hand. In order to develop an applied account of fairness in football, we need to investigate a number of contextual factors, such as the rules of the game, how it is typically played and many other contextual aspects. Let us further assume that the theorist in question has not pursued a specific investigation of the point and purpose of football. But the empiric investigations inform her, for example, about the conditions for winning and that most people playing the game aim to win. And she is also told, we may further assume, that some think that the aim is actually to have fun and to do your best, regardless of outcome. It so happens that in her view, comparably simple practices like football also have a number of competing ideas of their points and purposes, such that trying to settle which is the right one is a waste of time. Therefore, without further ado, after having performed the usual investigation of how football functions in theory and practice, she turns directly to the armchair and develops an account of fairness (Erman and Möller 2017a).

The account of fairness she returns with is this: fairness in football entails, for the player, never intentionally breaking the rules of the game and never acting like something has happened in any other way than how she believes it happened. Specifically, this entails never pretending to have been the victim of foul play when this is not the case (according to her belief).

Now, the question to be asked is if this account can be justified even though the theorist has failed to pay any attention to the point and purpose of football. Since we cannot see what such a study would add, normatively speaking, we cannot see how the answer could be 'no'. Once the theorist has all relevant contextual information, she can make the normative argument, utilising this information for developing and justifying her account.

A response we can anticipate, however, is the following: 'OK, the account can be justified, but this is because the theorist has in fact investigated the nature of the practice.' The thought here is that she knows, in effect, that the aim of the game is to win while following the set of rules in the football rulebook, which, *ex hypothesis*, is the point and purpose of football. Consequently, even though she has not directly interpreted the nature of football, in practice her investigation contains such information. Thus, her account can be justified only because she has in fact used a practice-dependent methodology.

The problem with this response is that it is either blatantly false or true in a way which dissolves the distinction between practice-dependent and practice-independent accounts. It is false in the sense that the theorist has not attempted to single out any determinate idea of the point and purpose of the game; she has merely, in her empirical investigation, received *statements* with approximately that content. She has formed no belief, justified or otherwise, about the point and purpose of the practice and thus cannot be said to know that the aim of the game is to win while following the set of rules in the football rulebook (as we have assumed to be the correct answer). What is true is that she has received what we assume to be information about the nature of the practice. But not only would accepting this as 'understanding the nature of the practice' conflate being given a statement that happens to be a true with *knowing* that the statement is true, it would just turn investigating the nature of the practice into something we *always* do when studying the context of a practice. Hence, it is not distinguishing a practice-dependent methodology from any other method for developing an applied guiding principle for a practice.

Consequently, even if we make the assumption that the point and purpose of football is to win in accordance with the rules, a theorist does not need to hold that belief to justify an account of fairness for football. Instead, as we will argue in Chapter 7, it seems that a sufficient constraint on a principle intended to guide this practice is that it must be *compatible* with the practice. This is the correlate to the traditional 'ought implies can' condition in moral philosophy: in order for an action to be morally prescribed, we must be able to perform it (in some relevant sense of 'able').

AN EPISTEMIC ARGUMENT FOR DEMOCRACY

Let us now turn to the third epistemological constraint found in the debates analysed, put forward in a number of articles and books by pragmatist epistemic theorists, such as Cheryl Misak and Robert Talisse (Misak 2000, 2008, 2009; Talisse 2005, 2007, 2009a, 2009b, 2010, 2014; Misak and Talisse 2014). The main claim of these theorists is that a certain form of democracy – deliberative democracy – is required given a set of fundamental epistemic premises which we cannot reasonably deny.

The motivation for the justificatory project of pragmatist epistemic theorists is dissatisfaction with mainstream accounts in liberal political theory. Despite their 'overlapping consensus' strategy, liberal accounts – such as Rawls' – cannot properly handle the fact of moral disagreement, according to pragmatist epistemic theorists. Democracy

requires consent, but at the same time citizens in pluralist societies (reasonably) disagree about their fundamental moral values.
Given such disagreement, it is not possible to offer a moral justification of democracy which is acceptable to all citizens. But since that is
what is required by democracy, democracy itself cannot be justified.
Talisse labels this problem 'the paradox of democratic justification',
and concludes that no moral justification of democracy can be successful (Talisse 2009a: Ch. 1 and 2).

The alternative strategy that pragmatist epistemic theorists pursue is
to justify democracy by a set of fundamental epistemic principles.[9] So,
while not giving up on the idea of appealing to *shared* values or commitments, these are not moral but epistemic. These epistemic principles
in turn entail a number of interpersonal epistemic commitments. From
these epistemic commitments, a commitment to democracy follows.
The argument explicitly appeals to internal coherence or rationality:
you cannot coherently reject democracy if you accept a set of fundamental epistemic principles.[10]

The approach has generally received positive reviews (Ball 2010;
May 2011; Saunders 2011; Lister 2011) and while we are largely sym-
pathetic to both the epistemic starting point and deliberative democracy, we will argue that the freestanding epistemic principles are too
weak to entail the suggested interpersonal epistemic commitments;
and even if these epistemic commitments are granted, they are still
insufficient to ground democracy (let alone democracy of a deliberative kind). Rather, we suggest epistemic arguments alone never suffice
to justify democracy: moral and other normative premises will always
be needed.

THE INFERENCE FROM EPISTEMIC PRINCIPLES TO
EPISTEMIC COMMITMENTS

As we could see above, the pragmatist epistemic argument for a free-
standing justification of democracy thus has a three-step structure: it
puts forward a number of fundamental epistemic principles, which we
cannot rationally deny (1). It then claims that a number of epistemic
commitments follow (2), which in turn justify deliberative democracy
(3). In this section we will argue against the inference from (1) to (2):
even if we grant the set of epistemic premises suggested by Misak and
Talisse, the epistemic commitments do not follow.

Misak and Talisse's fundamental epistemic principles revolve around the relationship between beliefs, reasons and truth. Misak's formulation of the epistemic principles focuses on what she labels two 'constitutive norms' of belief. The first norm is that beliefs aim at the truth; that is, we aim for our beliefs to be true (Misak 2004: 51). The second norm is about the relationship between an assertion and (potential) justification:

> When I believe p, I commit myself to saying what could speak for or against p and to giving up p in the face of sustained evidence and argument against it. A belief, in order to be a belief, is such that it is responsive to or answerable to reasons and evidence. (Misak 2004: 12)

Talisse formulates the epistemic principles in more detail, picking out five principles of what he calls 'folk epistemology':

P1. To believe some proposition, p, is to hold that p is true.
P2. To hold that p is true is generally to hold that the best reasons support p.
P3. To hold that p is supported by the best reasons is to hold that p is assertable.
P4. To assert that p is to enter into a social process of reason exchange.
P5. To engage in social processes of reason exchange is to at least implicitly adopt certain cognitive and dispositional norms related to one's epistemic character (Talisse 2009a: 87–8).

While Misak and Talisse's formulations are not identical, the differences do not matter for our argument; let us therefore refer to this combined set of principles and norms in what follows as 'fundamental epistemic principles' or simply 'epistemic principles'. As believers, Misak and Talisse argue, we are already committed to these principles; they are so basic that we simply cannot deny them. We basically agree with Misak and Talisse that we are rationally obliged to endorse these principles,[11] and in any case, for the sake of argument we will fully accept them here, since our aim is to show that even so, a commitment to democracy (let alone deliberative democracy) does not follow.

The problem for the pragmatist epistemic argument begins when Misak and Talisse go from the fundamental epistemic principles about our aim for truth and responsiveness to reason, to a set of epistemic commitments about our *search* for truth. Misak and Talisse put forward a number of epistemic commitments allegedly following from the fundamental epistemic principles. Misak's list of commitments include (Misak 2008: 103):

- Epistemic honesty: 'following reasons and evidence, rather than self-interest'
- Modesty: 'taking your views to be fallible'
- Charity: 'willingness to listen to the views of others'
- Integrity: 'willingness to uphold the deliberative process, no matter the difficulties encountered'

Talisse argues for a similar set of commitments, in particular focusing on the search for truth:

> [P]roper believing commits us to engaging with those whose experiences differ from our own; for if we are aiming at truth, we must seek out new and unfamiliar challenges. In this way, the norms of belief entail interpersonal norms of equality, participation, recognition, and inclusion. (Talisse 2014: 127)

These epistemic commitments constitute, on the pragmatist epistemic argument, an intersubjective 'middle-step' to a full-fledged commitment to democracy. And at first glance, thinking that they follow from the fundamental epistemic principles may seem reasonable. At least as heuristics to endorse in general, it seems reasonable that if we aim for our beliefs to be true, we should be responsive to input from others, and since our views are fallible and the search for truth is always an unfinished task, we should recognise the need for including further perspectives. But when Talisse and Misak elaborate on the epistemic commitments they take to follow from the fundamental principles, it becomes clear that they have something stronger in mind. Concerning the commitment to epistemic *inclusion*, Talisse explains that:

> proper believing requires not only that we tolerate criticism and persons with whom we disagree, but that we open ourselves to new challenges to our beliefs and new discursive partners; proper epistemic practice is in this way inherently epistemically *inclusive*.

Yet this inclusiveness is not based in a *moral* requirement to extend a respectful ear to all; its motivation is fully *epistemic*. Unless we take seriously the reasons and arguments of our critics, we are not doing our best with respect to the aim of having true beliefs. (Talisse 2009a: 124)

In a similar vein, epistemic *participation* is supposed to be incompatible not only with thinking that there is no need to consider objections for whatever reasons, but also with having 'consulted only those who also believe that p, and having considered only those reasons that confirm that p' (Talisse 2009a: 124). Our aim for truth is supposed to entail that we 'must seek out new and unfamiliar challenges' (Talisse 2014: 127). And as we saw above, *integrity* demands that we uphold the deliberative process 'no matter the difficulties encountered' (Misak 2008: 103).

Misak and Talisse's emphasis on the exception-less character of the epistemic commitments make them very demanding, but in view of their argumentative strategy, they have good internal reasons for insisting on such strong epistemic commitments. Since theirs is a coherence argument, ultimately claiming that anti-democrats are irrational *in their own light*, they need strong epistemic commitments. If the anti-democrat needs only to accept these commitments *prima facie*, the irrationality charge would not get off the ground, since she could then, without being internally incoherent, easily take there to be other reasons that trump these commitments.[12]

While strategically motivated, the strong reading of the epistemic commitments is what makes the overall argument face an uphill battle. Before moving to two distinct arguments against the inference from the epistemic principles to the epistemic commitments, let us give an example on how pre-theoretically unintuitive Misak and Talisse's epistemic commitments are.

Imagine the case of a brilliant electrical engineer, Dr Nicholas Tessla, who spends virtually all his time thinking about esoteric problems of semi-conducting. He is uninterested in questions of politics and most normative issues ranging from everyday conduct to justice and morality, apart from when they interfere with him being able to work on his research. In particular, since Dr Tessla is of the belief that what people generally talk about does not interest him, he avoids listening to the various groups on campus that try to get his attention. Whether right-wing propaganda, feminist activists or the group of ultra-nationalists who have started to hand out anti-refugee pamphlets, he quickly passes them by, never properly listening to them. In addition, when he has to teach and is (involuntarily) caught up in post-lecture conversation with an insistent student, he typically tries to end the discussion as soon as possible.

Now, Dr Tessla is certainly guilty of not listening to the arguments of all people. Nor is he seeking out new challenges outside the small area of electronics which interests him. From what we can tell, Dr Tessla may have quite a number of moral flaws. However, it seems to us without doubt that Tessla's neglect to seek, or even pay attention to, most of the claims of others is perfectly compatible with him being a *proper* believer in the sense of respecting the epistemic principles suggested by Misak and Talisse. We may easily assume, for example, that his beliefs 'do not resign when [he] properly assesses [his] reasons and evidence' (Talisse 2009b: 51). While he surely misses out on a lot of fun in life because he only focuses on work, he abides by the fundamental epistemic principles about the search for truth. It might be a narrower search than that of others, but it is a search all the same.

We believe the intuitive analysis of Dr. Tessla indicates what is wrong with the first inference of the pragmatist epistemic argument. While the fundamental epistemic premises about our *aim* for truth are sensible enough, and there is a corresponding sense in which we are all *searching* for truth, for the strong set of epistemic commitments to follow, our obligation to search for truth must be much stronger than what is reasonable. In the next section, we will present two arguments for why this is so.

LIMITS IN OUR SEARCH FOR TRUTH

The first argument for why the inference does not hold is that we have other concerns, against which our commitment to the search for truth needs to be balanced. One such concern is *moral*. In some circumstances, the search for truth may conflict with moral reasons against it, and then the moral reason may prove to be stronger. Let us say that Adam knows a few things that no one else knows. Now, *even if* torture is the only way to get that secret information out of Adam, our search for truth does not typically entail torturous acts. Indeed, the many ethical restrictions we put on science is a sign of our commitment to limit the search for truth. While we may disagree about the exact limits for when moral reasons trump other reasons in the search for a particular truth, the underlying intuition seems clear: we aim for truth, but not at all costs. This does not make us specious believers, but human ones.

Indeed, it seems clear to us that there are many cases where a search for truth is limited. Sometimes being sensitive to another's feelings means refraining from asking for further reasons even when an absolute aim for truth would require us to do so, for example in cases where we notice that they would rather not talk about the subject anymore. Likewise we should sometimes refrain from forcing reasons on people even when we think that they are misinformed. [13]

Does this mean that we should not accept the fundamental epistemic principles? No, since on a closer look, the commonsensical intuition that other concerns may trump a search for truth is perfectly consistent with the most reasonable reading of the epistemic principles. What we are committed to with the epistemic principles is to be *able* to give some reason for a belief that we hold, and that we abandon it if we are given what we take to be an overwhelming reason against it, and so on. But these modal commitments do not entail that we must constantly give reasons to others or listen to what they have to say.

This is fortunate, since epistemic premises which made such demands would in fact be self-contradictory, as our second argument will show. Constantly searching for the truth of every matter is in fact impossible. It is physically impossible, since no matter where we turn our attention, there are too many (potential) truths to investigate. Just sitting in his office, Dr Tessla would never get any work done at all, since he would never run out of truths to discover from looking around the room. Admittedly, Misak and Talisse have stressed that their focus is on belief maintenance and revision rather than belief acquisition (Misak and Talisse 2014: 369–70). But even if we 'only' focus on the beliefs that Dr Tessla happens to have, the task is insurmountable, since he would be obliged to constantly revise them in the manner demanded by the epistemic commitments. Indeed, due to the inferential and combinational nature of beliefs, it seems to be not only physically but also metaphysically impossible to search for all truths. There is simply an endless amount of facts out there.

Our belief revision process is thus by its nature limited, and in order to be able to function rationally, we also need heuristics to successfully navigate in our truth searching. If we stopped to count the grains of sand as soon as we came to the beach, we would not be able to do anything else for the rest of our lives. Thus, limiting our reason input in various ways is rational. The epistemic principles themselves address the issue of our obligations in light of evidence (given or demanded), but they are silent about which strategies we ought to employ for selecting among the endless set of truths to search for. Hence, while we may criticise Dr Tessla's selecting procedure for being too prejudiced, some filtering strategies are needed for epistemic reasons alone (in addition to other concerns, as mentioned in the previous argument). We need these strategies to find the time for our epistemic endeavours: those that are most important, that interest us the most or that we for some other reason set out to pursue. Fortunately, we are not epistemically obliged to continue the conversation with every person we meet, read every book someone hands to us or count the stars every time we go outside. The epistemic commitments put forward by pragmatist epistemic theorists neither follow from the epistemic principles, nor are they otherwise justified.

THE INFERENCE FROM EPISTEMIC COMMITMENTS TO DELIBERATIVE DEMOCRACY

Since the epistemic argument that we are rationally committed to democracy depends on the epistemic commitments we have just objected to, there is a sense in which the content of this section is redundant. Still, we think it is important to distinguish the epistemic commitments put forward, many of which are reasonable under somewhat weaker interpretations, from a full-fledged commitment to democracy. Hence, in this section we argue that even *given* a commitment to Misak and Talisse's epistemic commitments, a commitment to democracy does not follow.

Let us first note that the notion of democracy that pragmatist epistemic theorists take to be justified on purely epistemic grounds is far from a bare bones, Schumpeterian notion of democracy. While they endorse the formal properties of a liberal democracy as such (electoral procedures and so on), several deliberative aspects are added (Talisse 2009b: 49; Misak 2004: 15). Collective public reasoning, where citizens engage in reason exchange, takes centre stage in their account, decisions becoming binding precisely by being produced by processes reflecting proper epistemic practices (Talisse 2014: 126; Misak 2004: 15).

By holding beliefs, pragmatist epistemic theorists argue, we are committed to an epistemic endeavour which is social in nature. It requires participation among a community of inquirers, and this in turn entails a commitment to democracy: 'democracy is the political entailment – indeed the political *manifestation* – of the folk epistemic commitments each of us already endorse' (Talisse 2009a: 121). From our commitment to the 'interpersonal norms of equality, participation, recognition, and inclusion' (Talisse 2014: 127) emerges a commitment to a politics 'governed by familiar democratic norms of inclusion, equality, accountability, and participation' (Talisse 2009a: 124). Indeed, the full range of democratic norms arguably follows: the rights of free thought and expression, freedom of speech, open debate and open public spaces, freedom of information, and accountability (Talisse 2009a: 141–3, 2014: 127; Misak 2008: 95, 103).

While we agree that the *democratic* norms of equality, participation and inclusion are core concepts of democracy, we argue below that they do not follow from the *epistemic* commitments with the same labels.

Epistemic and Political Equality

The epistemic commitment to equality means that we are all equally entitled to voice our beliefs and our reasons for them. Talisse takes this to entail that we are 'epistemic peers', that is, equal participants in the epistemic enterprise, from which follows 'that we are equal citizens in the political community', where no citizens are seen as subordinates or subjects to arbitrary rule (Talisse 2009a: 124–5).

The move from epistemic peers to equal citizens in a political community is too fast, however. In democratic theory, political equality means something much more than that we are equally entitled to state our beliefs and engage in reason-giving. It also demands that we are equally entitled to influence the political decision-making. Support for this further property of democratic equality is fully lacking in the arguments of pragmatist epistemic theorists. And in fact it seems as if a community in which we have a complete set of rights to state our beliefs and argue for them (and against other beliefs) is fully compatible with having *no* formal say in the decision-making.

Indeed, there seem to exist many alternatives to democracy in organising a society politically in a way that respects the epistemic commitment to equality. Admittedly, as a matter of historical fact, non-democratic rule does not have a good track record in treating their citizens as equal participants in the epistemic enterprise, typically limiting freedom of speech and expression, freedom of conscience, freedom of information, a free media and the like. But conceptually, it is easy to imagine an expert rule or meritocracy where such freedoms and institutions are respected, but where political power is still distributed non-democratically, for example based on deliberative and intellectual talents and virtues. In part, there are historical examples along these lines. Napoleon admitted officers to the National Order of the Legion of Honour through scientific, artistic or military skilfulness and compe-tence rather than by wealth or ancestry (or at least attempted to do so). And John Stuart Mill, while believing in the free exchange of reasons and open debate, still defended the meritocratic idea of giving more votes to the educated (designed to give weight both to the value of diverse viewpoints and the value of wisdom; Mill 1859).

Epistemic and Democratic Participation

Epistemic participation demands that the agent not only engages in a free exchange of reasons, experience and arguments, but also that she actively includes as many perspectives as possible (Talisse 2009a: 124). Democratic participation, on the other hand, is foremost concerned with decision-making. Formally, it aims to secure that a sufficient num-ber of participants are involved in the political decision process. While both epistemic and democratic participation includes reason exchange, a truth-seeking inquiry is very different from practical decision-making. Similar to the previous case of epistemic equality, we may follow our commitment to participate actively in reason exchange, without having the power to impact the political decision-making. Or conversely, we may have the power to do so but choose not to.

Also, when it comes to informal aspects there is a gap between epistemic and democratic participation. For the deliberative democrat, public reasoning is essential (Habermas 1996). Contrary to the commit-ments of epistemic participation, where reaching the truth is the final aim, the endpoint of public reasoning is to act politically in the pub-lic sphere in order to identify social challenges, demand accountability of rule-makers and ensure that deliberative outcomes impact legally binding formal decision procedures. These aspects of political voice are different from aspiring to true belief. While the public space for the believer is an intersubjective social space (a space of reasons), it is also a political space for the democrat, where actions affect the agenda-setting (voice) as well as the decision-making (vote). We cannot achieve the latter solely by following the norms of belief; indeed, most believers do not raise their political voice by activities such as writing articles, demonstrating or engaging politically in other ways. Consequently, neither 'voice' nor 'vote' follows from the epistemic commitments.

Epistemic and Democratic Inclusion

A commitment to epistemic inclusion requires the agent to include (indeed seek out) the perspective of every other agent into her own deliberative process, in order to fulfil the aim of reaching true beliefs. This corresponds, pragmatist epistemic theorists argue, to the norm of democratic inclusion on the plausible presumption that the democratic method should 'ensure that the experiences of all are taken into consideration' (Misak 2008: 94). Decisions made by voting after open deliberation and discussion are valuable because such a 'deliberative democratic method is more likely to give us true or right or justified answers to our questions' (Misak 2008: 95.) Misak and Talisse further argue that an undemocratic process where an elite decides does not track truth as well as a democratic deliberative process, since we have no identifiable moral and political experts; therefore, the arguments and experience of every believer should ideally be taken into consideration in the search for truth on a political matter (Misak 2008: 102; Talisse 2009a: 124).[14]

While there seems to be a clear form of harmony or correspondence between the aim for truth and a process of including the perspective of everyone in a deliberative democratic process, on closer scrutiny the demands of epistemic and democratic inclusion diverge. In democratic inclusion, it is de facto not the case that the perspective of everyone is included, and the normative question of who *should* be included in the democratic decision-making, commonly known as the 'boundary problem', is one of the more discussed questions in political theory. There are two major responses to this problem in the debate: the so-called 'all affected interests principle' and the 'all subjected principle'. The former principle (roughly) states that all whose interests are significantly affected by a decision should have a say in the decision-making (Archibugi 1998; Shapiro 1999; Benhabib 2004; Goodin 2007), whereas the latter holds that all those who are subjected to the policies and laws should have a say in their making (Habermas 1996; Abizadeh 2012; Erman 2013, 2014). Neither of these two principles is justified on purely epistemic grounds, however. The all affected interests principle is justified by the egalitarian idea that people's fundamental interests should count equally, and the all subjected principle is grounded on the idea that people should be the authors of their own laws in order for the laws to be binding upon them. Hence, both are moral groundings in exactly the sense that pragmatist epistemic theorists reject.

As with the prior epistemic commitments, there is a justificatory gap between the norm of epistemic inclusion and the decision-making power coupled with the requirements of democratic inclusion. Let us say that we endorse the idea that democratic rule should 'take the views and experiences of all into account' (Misak 2008: 102). This idea has been suggested by several democratic theorists in recent years (see, for example, Dryzek and Niemeyer 2008). Still, this is compatible with not letting everyone be included in actual decision-making. In fact, it seems clear to us that including everyone would have counter-intuitive consequences from the standpoint of democracy (Erman 2013), since it would entail, for example, that US citizens must be included in the decision-making in China since they may have good arguments for how to best form a policy on workplace safety. Even if there are good reasons for including their *arguments* in the deliberation from the standpoint of truth-seeking, this does not entail a right to vote on the matter.

We conclude that neither the inference from epistemic principles to epistemic commitments nor the inference from epistemic commitments to democratic commitments is rationally obligatory in the morally free-standing way that pragmatist epistemic theorists claim. This does not mean, of course, that epistemic reasons cannot be part of an argument for democracy. If we successfully manage to argue (as some have attempted) that, in the long run, democracy is the best way of reaching truth, we would have a good reason for democracy, which together with other reasons for democracy could 'tip the scale' in its favour. But some of these other reasons, we are convinced, must be moral in character, since, in the end, the choice of system of rule is a matter of which normative principles we should follow.

NOTES

1. Sangiovanni calls them EU-S and EU-P, respectively (Sangiovanni 2016: 16–17), but we have changed the labels here to make them more intuitive (we think, at least).
2. In addition, he argues that mediated deduction, as opposed to the instrumental mode, need not aim for all-things-considered judgements; and that the relation between higher-level principles and applied principles is

that of a means to an end for the instrumental mode as opposed to a genus to a species for mediated deduction (Sangiovanni 2016: 17). See our objections to these specific claims (Erman and Möller 2017a).

3. This is indeed controversial as well, but let us for the sake of the argument grant it here.

4. Cf. Erman and Möller 2017a for doubts about this.

5. For a retributionist example, see Boonin 2008.

6. At least *pro tanto*. Strictly speaking, the utilitarian is against this type of compartmentalisation of the question, focusing on the general requirement that the act which is ultimately justified is that, and only that, which has the best consequences (in this case: best level of welfare).

7. Indeed, we may even imagine that her justificatory account includes this possibility as a hypothetical case (since we now assume that she has not specifically investigated the motivations of the participants) which she then argues against, in a similar way as we typically argue against whatever regrettable phenomenon we all too often witness in reality, such as racism, sexism and oppression.

8. We say perhaps, since investigating their values and motivations to determine their will may be said to put the cart before the horse.

9. While the full-fledged accounts of Misak and Talisse are far from identical, their individual works as well as their recent co-written paper demonstrate a shared commitment to the following coherence argument (cf. Talisse 2009a; Misak 2000; Misak and Talisse 2014).

10. Talisse and Misak sometimes express their position such that only *in* a democracy may we be genuine believers (e.g. Talisse 2009a: 122–3; Misak and Talisse 2014: 372), but with closer attention to their actual argument, it becomes clear that it is an argument for what it is rational to believe given certain premises – that is, a *coherence* argument (cf. e.g. Talisse 2009a: 122; Talisse 2009b: 51; Misak 2000: 46. See Erman and Möller 2016b for a more detailed analysis.)

11. In their defence of the fundamental epistemic principles, Misak and Talisse spend quite some space defending the notion of truth in politics. Since we are minimalists about truth, and happily accept that a political belief p may be true, as well as that we may have better or worse reasons for believing p, we have no qualms about (P1). In our opinion, Talisse's (P4) and (P5) are potential weak spots. But, as we state in the main text, we leave these potential worries alone, and gladly accept these fundamental epistemic principles in what follows.

12. Misak and Talisse also object to another weaker interpretation of the epistemic commitments: that it is *doubt* about a belief that commits a person to further inquiry (see e.g. Sleat 2009: 55–6; MacGilvray 2014: 110–14). In their recent co-written reply to critics, they deny this interpretation, however, stressing that 'to [satisfy the constitutive doxastic

norms] we obviously have to hear what the opponents say, what reasons they have to offer' (Misak and Talisse 2014: 370).

13. See Tsai 2014 for further arguments for when reason insistence may display a lack of respect for the other person.

14. While we do not go into the topic in detail here (but see Erman and Möller 2016b), the presumption that there are no moral experts strikes us as both implausible and irrelevant. It is implausible since there seem to be people with better and worse arguments in the moral and political sphere just as in any other, and it is irrelevant since it is at least *conceivable* that a person could hold that there are such experts. Given such a belief (true or false), it is not irrational to also believe that they should decide more in matters of politics. But Misak and Talisse need it to be so in order for the argument to go through as a coherence argument.

Chapter 6

POLITICAL CONSTRAINTS

This chapter examines arguments for how political practices condition normative political principles. Such arguments have been made by practice-dependent theorists in the global justice debate and by political realists in the debate on political legitimacy. In the latter debate, realists argue that principles of political legitimacy must be theorised from 'within' the political, focusing on the actual institutions, practices and processes through which citizens address shared problems in their society. In the former debate, practice-dependent theorists argue that institutionally mediated relationships condition appropriate criteria of justice and that justice therefore must be theorised from the workings of actual institutions.

Even though there has been little or no exchange between these two debates, several premises are shared and would benefit from systematic scrutiny. This chapter presents and critically examines both arguments for political constraints on normative political principles. With regard to political realism, we demonstrate that the core question in the realist critique of political moralism concerns which justificatory domain ought to have primacy in deciding what political legitimacy is, and thus different forms of constraints on reasons in support of a principle of political legitimacy (e.g. political or moral reasons or both). It is argued that realists are wrong to claim that political moralism sees morality as something prior to or external to politics. Concerning the positive arguments put forward by realists, we argue that none of their justificatory strategies that allegedly put political constraints on normative political principles holds.

With regard to practice-dependent theorists focusing on political constraints in the form of institutions, a similar scepticism is raised against the primacy of institutions in deciding what justice is. The chapter analyses a weaker and a stronger interpretation of institutional practice-dependence. It is argued that the weaker interpretation is reasonable but does not imply that the choice between practice-dependence and practice-independence has wide-ranging implications for the content and justification of justice, as practice-dependent theorists claim. On the stronger interpretation, a de facto dichotomy between practice-dependence and practice-independence is established, but this is, we argue, at the price of being unreasonable.

WHAT IS SO SPECIAL ABOUT THE POLITICAL?

Political realism has become an influential approach in the current debate on political legitimacy and democracy. While it is fair to say that it is not yet a unified position, realists share enough assumptions to constitute an alternative approach to mainstream political theory.[1] First, realists unite with non-ideal theorists in the assumption that the idealism and moralism of mainstream accounts make them inadequate: since they do not have practical import, they are irrelevant as political theories. Second, realists assume that any plausible political theory must see legitimacy as distinctly political in the sense that it utilises normative sources 'within' the political rather than from some external moral standpoint.

As mentioned in Chapter 2, political realists reject what they call the 'ethics first' premise of political moralism. According to this premise, morality is given priority over politics and the political domain is seen mainly as an arena for the application of moral principles. The models incorporating the ethics first premise assume that political practices are either intended to express moral principles, ideals and values or offer external constraints on what politics can rightfully do (Williams 2005: 1–2; Rossi 2012: 151). In both models, political theorising starts from 'outside' politics such that the demands of morality give content to principles of political legitimacy (Sleat 2010: 486). Apart from claiming that moralists theorise political legitimacy from an external moral standpoint, realists further argue that the ethics first premise implies that morality is seen as prior to politics, which means that political legitimacy is theorised as a pre-political concept, through which politics is cleansed by prior moral reasoning (Williams 2005: 1–2; Rossi 2012: 151). According to realists, this leads to erroneous principles of political legitimacy (Sleat 2010; Bellamy 2010; Geuss 2008; Williams 2005; Galston 2010; Horton 2010; cf. Erman and Möller 2015a: 216). Consensus on some moral values prior and external to politics, realists argue, cannot be achieved, since it is only through the exercise of political power that any agreement is possible. Therefore, any plausible account of political legitimacy must be justified using normative sources from within politics itself.

In a nutshell, the justification for why normative political principles should be theorised from within politics rather than from a moral standpoint on the outside, hence being delimited by distinctly political practices, has a negative (critical) and a positive (constructive) side. Below, we first take a look at the realist critique of the ethics first premise, and then analyse the positive arguments in defence of political constraints on principles.

THE REALIST CRITIQUE OF THE ETHICS FIRST PREMISE

As we saw above, realists claim that the ethics first premise leads to flawed conceptions of political legitimacy. However, it is far from clear how the ethics first premise should be understood, that is, in what sense morality is supposed to be prior and external to politics, as realists claim. Before analysing possible realist interpretations, we need to know more about how realists characterise the political and moral domains. While very little is said about what they see as the distinctive properties of each domain, realists seem to rely on a fairly commonsensical view. On this view, morality is primarily about how individuals ought to live their lives and distinguish right from wrong, good from bad and so on, whereas politics is primarily about how individuals ought to live together on the societal level and engage in collective action and decision-making. As will be discussed below, politics for realists consists of social relations involving authority and power (Sleat 2010; Bellamy 2010; Newey 2010).

Against the backdrop of this broad characterisation, how is the ethics first premise supposed to be understood? As far as we can tell, in neither of the interpretations hinted at by realists does it make sense to say that morality is prior and external to politics. To begin with, if this priority is supposed to be interpreted in epistemological terms, it seems to be too strong a claim, since we are able to understand and gain knowledge of politics without prior knowledge about morality. A conceptual reading seems equally problematic, since there is little to suggest that political concepts presuppose moral concepts such that one cannot understand politics by grasping what governments and parliaments do, what collective decision-making is, how accountability mechanisms function and so on. On yet another interpretation, 'prior to' is to be interpreted in temporal, presumably causal, terms. But this idea is also doubtful, because it would suggest that morality always comes first and somehow causes politics to occur (Erman and Möller 2015a: 225). Even if we can imagine examples where this is the case, such as when people demand that certain moral rights should be legislated to become international human rights, this is far from always the case. In a situation in which people encounter a collective action problem, for example, political rather than moral concerns are often the initiating force. In fact, even in cases where a moral demand is raised, this may emerge in a political situation rather than having any prior and external force.

Hence, while it is primarily the alleged falsity of the ethics first premise that leads realists to reject mainstream (moralist) accounts and justifies the requirement to use normative sources solely from within the political domain, it is difficult to grasp what the ethics first premise is supposed to entail on their reading. As we have seen, the claim that it entails that morality is prior and external to politics, understood epistemologically, conceptually, temporally or causally, seems implausible.[2]

Let us therefore put aside the problems encountered by realists in their attempt to make sense of (and reject) the ethics first premise to justify the primacy of politics in theorising normative political principles, and instead take a closer look at the positive part of the justification, namely realists' own substantive arguments for this primacy. Rather than setting up an artificial and stylised moral choice situation in which the hypothetical parties are assumed to reach consensus on proper normative political principles, realists start out from the assumption that deep disagreement and insoluble conflict is an inevitable part of politics and therefore something that any account of legitimacy must take seriously. The two main justificatory strategies employed by realists to argue for the primacy of politics, and the requirement that only normative sources available within the political are allowed, refer to the constitutive features of politics and the concept of politics, respectively. Let us have a look at each strategy in turn.

NORMATIVE POLITICAL PRINCIPLES AND THE CONSTITUTIVE FEATURES OF POLITICS

A common assumption among realists is that any plausible account of political legitimacy must respect the constitutive features of politics. For realists, politics is foremost concerned with the maintenance of stability and order, and to finding ways to live together and organise society in light of insoluble moral disagreement and conflicts of interest. Apart from disagreement and conflict, other constitutive features stressed by realists include authority, gaining and maintaining political power, coercion and the monopoly of violence (Jubb 2015a: 679, 2015b: 919–21; Galston 2010: 408; Sleat forthcoming). From this viewpoint, moralism is flawed because it fails to grasp what politics is and in doing so it fails to adjust its 'prescriptions to the constraints of real politics, rather than the other way around' (Rossi 2013: 558). Since authority, coercion, conflict, disagreement and so on are constitutive features of politics, they 'ought to be taken as given or fixed points in any philosophy of politics' (Sleat forthcoming).

In view of our focus in this chapter on political constraints, we must ask: what does it mean for realists to respect these features of politics? For realists, it entails a restriction which commonly takes the form of a 'compatibility constraint', stating that a justified account of political legitimacy must be consistent with the constitutive features of politics (Sleat forthcoming). This constraint does not constitute a first-order claim that points directly to a specific substantive condition of legitimacy. Rather, it takes the form of a metatheoretical claim which delimits the content of principles or standards of legitimacy by requiring that such standards and principles cannot assume for their justification, or must not entail, features that are not compatible with the constitutive features of politics (Erman and Möller forthcoming).

There are two arguments put forward by realists to support the compatibility constraint, one positive and one negative. We will argue that neither of them holds. But before doing so, let us just stress that our argument here is independent of the justificatory status of the constitutive features of politics listed by realists. While we treat them as correct for the sake of argument however, it is worth noting that these suggestions are highly controversial. More importantly, they are also unsubstantiated and seem to mirror actual features of political practices rather than necessary features. For example, it seems premature to think that we have established that disagreement is a constitutive feature of politics until we have a convincing account of the impossibility of agreement. For sure, we have not yet witnessed a very large group of people reach full agreement after due deliberation. But this does not establish the impossibility of such an agreement. Moreover, history is full of examples – women's liberation movement, universal suffrage, the end of slavery and so on – where new political practices have emerged that were conceived of as impossible by contemporary fellow citizens.

The positive argument for the compatibility constraint relies on yet another metatheoretical constraint, which is general in nature but which applied to politics allegedly lends support to the compatibility constraint. We call this the 'theory constraint' since it states that, necessarily, a theory that is not consistent with the constitutive features of a phenomenon is not a theory of that phenomenon. Although realists generally take the truth of the theory constraint for granted, Matt Sleat has offered an elaborate defence of it through a number of examples. In one of the examples, Sleat imagines a scientist who comes up with a theory of the reactive properties of hydrogen. The problem with this theory is that it works only if we assume that hydrogen has two protons in its nucleus, rather than one. Sleat infers that this is not an adequate theory of its subject matter since it neglects the constitutive features of the phenomenon in question. Hence, it is not only a bad theory of hydrogen; it is not a theory *about* hydrogen at all (Sleat forthcoming).

The problem with this example is that seems to undermine rather than provide support for the theory constraint and, by extension, the compatibility constraint. This can be shown by looking at the well-known philosophical problem of establishing a clear distinction between saying something *false* about a subject matter and talking about another subject matter. In a trivial sense, it is of course true that the scientist's theory cannot be a justified theory about hydrogen given that one proton in the nucleus is a defining feature of hydrogen. But if we take a look at the history of science, it is full of examples of how scientists have changed their ideas of what is required for belonging to a certain kind. A famous example is atoms, which were originally thought to be the smallest particle in universe (hence the name which in ancient Greek means 'indivisible'). When scientists later on discovered that what they had called 'atoms' were in fact not the smallest particle but consisted of even smaller elements, they did not say that they did not talk about atoms anymore. Rather, they said that they had falsely believed that atoms were indivisible. The same is the case with electrons, which were initially thought to be positively charged particles, but were later on revealed to be negatively charged.

If we move from the natural sciences to value sciences, we usually require even less overlap of (natural) properties for accepting that a belief purportedly about X is in fact a belief about X. Say that Anna believes that the property of moral rightness consists of treating others as ends in themselves. Even if John is convinced that it instead consists in the property of maximising well-being, we typically do not conclude that their theories are about different phenomena. Rather, we see them as having different theories about the same subject matter, namely, moral rightness.[3] The same is true of the phenomenon of politics, where we typically categorise a very broad spectrum of orders as 'political orders' and consider a very broad spectrum of practices to be 'political practices'. In view of this, there seems to be plenty of room for categorising a theory as about the subject matter sought, regardless of what the factual status of the properties of the theory happens to be. Hence, we conclude that the theory constraint does not hold and therefore cannot lend support to the compatibility constraint (Erman and Möller forthcoming).

The second argument for the compatibility constraint is negative in that it aims to undermine positive arguments against it rather than directly seeking to support it. The most detailed elaboration of this argument is made by Sleat in an attempt to reject a claim made by David Estlund (2014). In line with our inquiry in this chapter, Estlund considers whether an account that includes assumptions that are incompatible with the necessary characteristics of politics would contain a fatal flaw. In his example, he assumes moral flawlessness and considers a political theory that offered a compelling argument for why a society could not be characterised as legitimate or just in conditions such as the constitutive features of politics stressed by realists. On the realist definition of politics, it would not be a political theory. But, Estlund argues, this then just becomes a definitional question, since even if it does not count as a political theory under this definition, 'this would leave entirely intact its claim to have the correct theory of justice, authority, and legitimacy' (Estlund 2014: 131).

Sleat interprets Estlund to be saying that it 'is no defect of a political theory if it does not take adequate account of the nature of politics' (Sleat forthcoming). And this is precisely why the argument is flawed, according to Sleat, since the theory fails to be a theory of politics at all. But this interpretation misses Estlund's point. The basic premise in Estlund's argument is that it *grants* the realist claim that a political theory must be compatible with the constitutive features of politics and that the theory he has in mind could thus not be counted as a political theory. Estlund's central point, instead, is that it may still be the appropriate normative theory for a society. One cannot reject a normative theory which offers persuasive arguments for why legitimacy in a society is incompatible with, for example, disagreement, on the ground that it would not then be a *political* theory. If it is a compelling theory and possible to implement in a society, it does not matter for its normative status whether it is called political or not.

The central normative question in the debate in which realists typically engage is what normative theory of legitimacy is justified for a society. And if the political domain is defined such that some societies for which it is meaningful to talk about legitimacy do not become part of the political, so much the worse for 'the political'. The hydrogen example brought forward by Sleat actually illustrates precisely this point. In describing this case, Sleat claims that even if the theory suggested were otherwise faultless, 'we would nevertheless insist that it is still a bad theory' since the hydrogen atom only has one proton in its nucleus and the theory only works under the assumption that hydrogen has two protons, two neutrons and two electrons (Sleat forthcoming). But we find this to be an inaccurate way of describing the theory. Because rather than being a bad theory about hydrogen, it would be more appropriately classified as a faultless theory about the reactive properties of helium-4, the isotope of helium which carries exactly two protons, two neutrons and two electrons. While this theory would not be very helpful to the person who is interested in the reactive properties of hydrogen, it would be extremely helpful to the person who tries to find a gas to use in the balloons for her daughter's birthday party. For it would tell her that the reactive properties of the 'hydrogen' in the theory suggested (actually, helium-4) make it much more suitable than proper hydrogen. The scientist's findings in Sleat's example would in other words have been very helpful pre-Hindenburg (Erman and Möller forthcoming).

In sum, realists have tried to make the case that normative political principles are constrained by political practices by arguing that any plausible theory must be consistent with the constitutive features of politics (the compatibility constraint). We have tried to show why the two arguments offered in support of this constraint fail.

NORMATIVE POLITICAL PRINCIPLES AND THE CONCEPT OF POLITICS

Apart from utilising the constitutive features of politics to argue that political practices constrain normative political principles, realists also have adopted a justificatory strategy relying on the concept of politics. Several realists in the debate argue that the concept of politics may ground a normative account of political legitimacy (Rossi and Sleat 2014; Jubb and Rossi 2015; Sleat 2010). For them, Bernard Williams' conceptual distinction between 'politics' and 'sheer domination' is seen as providing a normative basis for political legitimacy. Since this distinction adds a normative dimension to our understanding of politics, the argument goes, no sources of normativity external to politics are needed to theorise legitimacy (Hall 2017; Sleat 2010; Jubb and Rossi 2015).

To support this idea, realists use the normative status of the concept of politics, stressing that politics is a so-called 'thick evaluative concept', similar to concepts such as 'kind', 'cruel' and 'brave'. What is characteristic of a thick evaluative concept is that it is neither exclusively normative like 'thin' evaluative concepts (good, right), nor exclusively descriptive like 'thin' non-normative concepts (rivers, chairs). Rather, comprehending a thick evaluative concept requires that we grasp both its descriptive and evaluative content. Consider the paradigmatic example of bravery. This concept requires both that we understand what it entails, such as promoting a valued aim in a dangerous situation, and that we understand that it is something positive (sometimes called its 'good-making' property).[4] The realist idea here is that since there is an evaluative aspect intrinsic to the concept of politics, we do not need to refer to any additional values (such as the value of self-ownership or autonomy) to justify that 'might is not right'. Competent users of the notion of politics, *qua* competent users, already grasp that politics is distinct from sheer domination (Rossi and Sleat 2014: 693; Jubb and Rossi 2015: 455–8; see also Williams 1985: 140–2).

We do not see how the concept of politics can be drawn upon to argue for political constraints on normative political principles. First, a conceptual distinction does not imply incompatibility. Certainly, politics and sheer domination are distinct concepts, but this does not entail that a state of domination cannot be political. A train and blueness are certainly distinct, but a train may be blue nevertheless. The same is true of thick concepts. 'Kindness' and 'cruelty' are typical thick concepts, and a person or action may be both kind (positive valence) and cruel (negative valence). In other words, we can fully understand the negative valence of domination, such as in the case of slavery, but argue, say, that the practices of slavery are legitimate nonetheless (Erman and Möller 2015a, 2015d). In fact, this is most likely how many slave owners justified their practice.

Hence, that two concepts are distinct is not helpful for the theorist who wishes to argue for political constraints on principles utilising the concept of politics. For one concept (politics) to 'ban' another concept (domination), it must be a conceptual truth that the concepts are not merely distinct but incompatible. If so, the notion of politics, *qua* notion, would be normatively effective in the sense that for a given practice, the theorist may ask if it counts as a political practice. If not, that practice cannot be a legitimate political practice. However, the only way that the notion itself may offer necessary and sufficient conditions for legitimacy is if politics and legitimate politics mean the same thing. And it seems clear that they do not, since a state of politics may be illegitimate and still count as political.

Of course, we may give terms broad or narrow interpretations. If realists would go for a broad interpretation of politics, which is the commonsensical one both in political theory and in colloquial usage, orders with a varying degree of legitimacy would count as political orders. From this viewpoint, however, the normative force of the notion of politics becomes very weak, since most assertions that are claimed to be about politics can intelligibly be grasped as such, whether we agree with them or not. As history has shown, many have regarded practices of slavery to be compatible with legitimacy. Similarly, many political orders in our current world are considered to be illegitimate. In view of the broad interpretation of politics, the case for excluding these orders as non-political seems weak indeed.

On the other hand, if realists instead go for a very narrow interpretation of politics, which equated politics with legitimate politics, the notion would allow only a small subset of what we usually consider to be political orders to be truly political. But this would not help realists' case at all, for two reasons. First, an important aspect of the realist project is to stress the many ways in which politics is 'dirty' and much more Machiavellian in nature than assumed by mainstream theorists. But this aspect is difficult to combine with a very narrow (and relatively optimistic) notion of politics. Second, and more importantly, while giving the term a narrow interpretation would indeed assist in grounding an account of legitimacy on *that* very notion of politics, this would shift rather than solve the question at hand. For if we define politics as legitimate politics, we simply shift the original question 'which political orders are legitimate?' to the question 'which orders are political?' And this question is just as controversial as the original one. Arguably, to claim that a notion of legitimate politics is not right because it does not count as politics hardly constitutes an argument.[5]

Against the justificatory strategy using the concept of politics to argue for political constraints on normative political principles, we conclude that the question of which principles of legitimacy should regulate a practice (or demand that the practice should be eradicated) must be answered on *substantial* rather than conceptual grounds, however thick the concepts involved.

WHAT IS SO SPECIAL ABOUT INSTITUTIONS?

If realists stress the primacy of politics in theorising principles of legitimacy, some practice-dependent theorists have stressed the primacy of institutions in theorising principles of justice. Practice-dependent theorists, as we have seen, argue that social and political practices fundamentally affect principles of justice. As mentioned in Chapter 2, they all accept Sangiovanni's practice-dependence thesis, which states that 'the content, scope, and justification of a conception of justice depend on the structure and form of the practices that the conception is intended to govern' (Sangiovanni 2008: 138; James 2012: 30, 2005: 283–4; Banai et al. 2011: 49; Rossi 2012: 159). They also argue that this thesis is denied by practice-independent theorists, which has important implications, since the choice between practice-dependence and practice-independence essentially shapes 'how one conceives of the nature of justice' (Sangiovanni 2008: 140). Apart from this general thesis about the role of practices, some theorists focus particularly on institutionalised practices. Sangiovanni, for example, concludes that a focus on institutions reveals that principles of justice take an international rather than cosmopolitan form (Sangiovanni 2008).

Apart from a commitment to the practice-dependence thesis and to the interpretive practice-based methodology discussed in previous chapters, the institutional version of practice-dependence stresses the importance of institutions for mediating and altering the relations between people. On this view, institutions do not merely matter for the application of principles of justice but also for their content and justification, since institutions put people in a special relation to each other, the nature of which is such that it 'gives rise to first principles of justice that would not have existed otherwise' (Sangiovanni 2008: 140).

Sangiovanni contrasts the institutional version of the practice-dependent approach from what he calls the 'cultural conventionalist' version, defended for example by Michael Walzer (1983, 1987). According to Sangiovanni, the justice of an institutional system on a cultural conventionalist view is to be assessed by its relation to criteria implicit in the cultural practices sustaining it. In order to be just, a system must thus embody and implement the values that are already contained in the practices in question. While institutional practice-dependence would agree that the content of principles of justice will depend on the context they are intended to regulate, it would, however, deny that the existence of a culture is 'either necessary or sufficient for justice to apply' (Sangiovanni 2008: 146). Further, it would not require us to comply with any principle that could be directly derived from a specific self-understanding. Instead, the proponent of institutional practice-dependence claims that institutionally mediated relationships condition rather than determine appropriate criteria of justice (Sangiovanni 2008: 147).

WEAKER AND STRONGER INTERPRETATIONS OF INSTITUTIONAL PRACTICE-DEPENDENCE

The institutional version of practice-dependence thus assumes that practices from which we derive principles of justice must be actual and institutionally mediated.[6] For the sake of simplicity, let us call the two components of the practices from which these principles are supposed to be derived the 'actuality requirement' and the 'institutional requirement'. Now, while these requirements are often alluded to, what they entail is not fully clear. Let us therefore distinguish between a weaker and a stronger interpretation of them.

Consider first the actuality requirement. On a weak interpretation, the requirement is an application of Wittgensteinian rule-following ideas: the claim that practices which must be actual in order for a principle to be justified refers to the *background practices* in light of which the principle is to be understood. As we argued in Chapter 3, Wittgenstein's idea that a rule or principle only has determinate meaning given a background practice – a way of applying it that is implicit in the practice – seems sensible indeed (Wittgenstein 1953). The problem is that this idea cannot be invoked to chisel out a difference between a practice-independent principle disconnected from 'the actual' and a practice-dependent principle derived from it, since this is true of *all* principles. Such a move would thus be based on a misguided overextension of Wittgenstein's basic point. In particular, Wittgenstein's insight does not support the idea that practice-independent principles lack content whereas practice-dependent principles do not, based on the thought that only the latter are formulated under actual real world circumstances. If that were true, it would entail that practice-independent theorists formulate their principles in a vacuum, isolated from the practical application of the terms they use. But practice-independent theorists are not imaginary agents. Their propositions are asserted publicly just as much as propositions made by practice-dependent theorists, and in the relevant sense of the expression, they are both sharing a 'form of life' with the rest of us (Wittgenstein 1953: §241). Indeed, the very example Wittgenstein uses in *Philosophical Investigations* to illustrate his point – the correct application of mathematical terms – is ideal and practice-independent, which clearly indicates that his point is not about abstract practice-independent principles, on the one hand, and concrete application, on the other, but about the need for a background practice in which the very notion of acting in accordance with a principle can get a grip (McDowell 1984).

Consequently, interpreted in weak terms, we see no reason why practice-independent theorists must deny the essential role of actual practices for theorising normative political principles.

Now, consider the institutional requirement. On a weak interpretation, this requirement would state that justice should foremost be concerned with institutions and institutional structures. However, similar to the weak interpretation of the actuality requirement, this demand would not single out a practice-dependent approach. Quite the opposite. In the debate on global justice, the focus on the basic structure of society and on institutionalised schemes of cooperation seems shared among cosmopolitan, liberal and statist theorists (Nagel 2005; Ypi 2008; Pogge 2002; Caney 2006; Moellendorf 2011). They could all subscribe to Sangiovanni's claim that the relationship between institutions and persons are special in the sense that institutions establish certain networks of relationships among people, a set of background conditions that 'alters the way in which participants interact', which, in turn, shapes the reasons people might have for endorsing certain principles of justice (Sangiovanni 2008: 147).

In sum, both practice-independent and practice-dependent theorists would acknowledge the importance of actual practices in the minimal sense portrayed above, as well as the central role ascribed to institutions. Hence, on a weak interpretation, no particular political constraints are put on normative political principles from a practice-based view in comparison to mainstream political theory. It is quite clear, however, that proponents of the institutional version of practice-dependence must have something stronger in mind since they want to argue that the choice between practice-dependence and practice-independence has wide-ranging implications for justice. As we discussed in some detail in Chapter 5, it is repeatedly argued that we must look at the point and purpose of specific and presently existing institutions and the ways in which they put actual people in a specific relationship and shape their factual reasons for endorsing certain principles of justice, in order to derive appropriate criteria of justice (Sangiovanni 2008; Rossi 2012; Ronzoni 2009).[7] However, even if such a strong interpretation of the two requirements would most likely establish a de facto dichotomy between practice-independent and practice-dependent views in the sense that we will find no practice-independent account supporting it, it seems unreasonable to limit our normative theorising in this way.

It is one thing to claim that through a neglect of actual institutional practices we run the risk of abstracting away relations of coercion and domination that should not be neglected in normative theory, but quite another to claim that a principle of justice can *only* get determinate content and justification by understanding specific instances of such actual institutions here and now. While the former implies that experiences from the world play a hermeneutic, motivating and justificatory role when principles of justice are developed, the latter implies that such principles can only emerge given certain properties of the world as it is in the present. But why should such contingent facts have that kind of veto power over justice? As discussed earlier, suppose that we found no present institutions whose point and purpose was to protect against gender inequalities. Why would a theory that demands that a just society *should* be gender equal for this reason be flawed, if it is freed from this accusation were there but one such institution?

Interestingly, Sangiovanni does not offer any justification for restricting justice *only* to institutionally mediated relations. While it is certainly true that institutions shape the social relationships among people in relevant ways, other things do that too. Even if it were the case that institutionally mediated relations shape our reasons for endorsing principles of justice more than anything else, it does not follow that other kinds of relationships are irrelevant and not to be taken into account. Moreover, a problem with restricting the definition of justice to institutionalised contexts is that the question of justice then does not even arise outside such contexts. Consider, for example, non-institutionalised relations of domination. If justice is concerned with the abolishment of arbitrary rule, it might be the case that justice demands the establishment of certain institutions rather than taking institutions as a premise (see Forst 2011). Sangiovanni's answer must be that as long as such relations are not institutionally mediated, they are not a task for justice. But he offers no justification for such a counter-intuitive restriction. Perhaps there is a tacit Rawlsian presumption here that major domestic institutions constitute the most basic of existing social structures because their effects are so profound (Rawls 1971; James 2005: 298). However, this still leaves open the question why such a priority of institutions would restrict justice such that institutionally mediated practices are the *only* sources of problems and claims of justice (cf. Meckled-Garcia 2008).

In fact, when illustrating his institutional version of the practice-dependent approach, Sangiovanni considers Rawls' account of fairness since the early 1980s to be a paradigmatic example. In his reading, Rawls' principles of justice are arrived at from a specific political self-understanding of liberal constitutional democracies, justified through an appeal to interpretive facts about the history and traditions embedded in the public life of such societies. In other words, the content, scope and justification of a conception of justice are determined 'in terms of the function that justice intended to play within the social and political institutions of a constitutional democracy' (Sangiovanni 2008: 151).

If this reading is correct, we cannot see how Rawls would be an example of institutional practice-dependence, since justice as fairness does not demand Sangiovanni's strong requirement of (at least) an actually existing institution or set of institutions, but rather seems to have a *kind* of institution in mind, which possesses certain abstract characteristics (Rawls 1993, 1999). And this for good reasons, because surely it would be a weakness of Rawls' theory if justice as fairness would cease to apply if we found one institution within an existing constitutional democracy which did not fully match all criteria (all correct 'interpretive facts', as it were) or if an atom bomb destroyed all presently existing constitutional democracies. Neither could it ever apply to a fictitious liberal constitutional democracy in a novel or a movie.[8]

An additional problem with Sangiovanni's insistence on a strong interpretation of the two requirements has to do with the fact that his practice-dependent account, as we discussed in Chapter 4, recognises

the importance of reflective equilibrium in its interpretive methodology, in line with Rawls. Even if one might get the impression from
the practice-based methodology that the move from interpretation
to derivation of justified first principles is supposed to be understood
as a one-way story, on closer inspection this is not the case. Instead,
Sangiovanni stresses that the success of an interpretation is supposed
to be judged in light of the theory *as a whole,* 'including the principles of
justice ultimately derived from it' (2008: 149, n. 28). Indeed, one of the
attractive features of such a dialectic understanding of the relationship
between our considered judgements about the rules that we believe
govern particular cases and more general theoretical or principled considerations is that it acknowledges human reason as a self-reflective
and self-critical faculty.

Sangiovanni's acknowledgment of reflective equilibrium as a property of the practice-based interpretive methodology, however, gives us
yet another reason to question the plausibility and desirability of the
strong reading of the requirements. Because why would we need a specific, actually existing institution in order to elaborate principles of justice
through such a reflective approach? Even if we granted the importance
of knowing points of purposes (which we strongly questioned in the
previous chapter), all we seem to need here is to know the point and
purpose of the *kind* of institution that the principles of justice are supposed to govern, and the role that these principles are supposed to play;
or, alternatively, the *desired* point and purpose of such institutions, and
the *desired* role of the principles. We need neither actual specific existing
institutions nor actual purposes and functions.[9]

INSTITUTIONALISED PRACTICES AND THE SCOPE OF JUSTICE

The main motivation behind the emergence of the practice-dependent
approach can be traced to the concern about the scope of justice. Practice-dependent theorists have set out to expose a tension or gap in the
mainstream liberal tradition between egalitarian principles of universal
scope, on the one hand, and their limited application within a particular
territorial unit, on the other. In their view, practice-independent conceptions of global justice have neglected this gap by simply presuming
that the content and justification of principles of justice and where they
are supposed to be realised are two independent questions. By contrast,
practice-dependent theorists wish to show that once we investigate
this gap and the relationship between these two questions, theorising

cosmopolitan principles of justice becomes a much more problematic enterprise. A common assumption seems to be that a practice-dependent approach gives us reason to be sceptical of global justice, even if it does not, strictly speaking, entail this (Nagel 2005; Sangiovanni 2008; James 2012; Ronzoni 2009). If we adopt a practice-independent stance, on the other hand, we will most likely support principles with global scope, wrongly deriving such principles from an egalitarian principle of some sort (Sangiovanni 2008: 140).

In light of our argument so far, we doubt that this diagnosis about the scope of justice is correct. We have made the case that under a reasonable weaker reading of the actuality requirement and the institutional requirement, a practice-dependent account does not give us any privileged hermeneutic or justificatory position vis-à-vis the practice-independent account for theorising normative political principles in the world of beliefs, values and practices. Instead, on this weaker reading, a practice-independent account seems compatible with the basic presumptions of a practice-dependent account. Therefore, contrary to what practice-dependent theorists presume, the choice between them does not seem to tell us much about the scope of justice.

Interestingly, not even Sangiovanni's strong reading of the two requirements seems equipped to do so. Let us for the sake of argument presume that justice must necessarily be conditioned by actual and institutionally mediated practices and that we can only derive principles of justice through the practice-based interpretive methodology. Whether we end up justifying or refuting cosmopolitan principles of justice will still be dependent on which institutions we strive to get interpretive facts about and how general we interpret their point and purpose, as well as the role the regulative principles are supposed to play. For example, if we choose to take a look at a set of global institutions and interpret its point and purpose in terms of protecting basic human interests, it might be the case that we derive cosmopolitan principles from these interpretive facts. In fact, we cannot exclude the possibility that we will end up with one principle of justice applicable to local, regional, national and global institutions alike, all depending on how broadly we interpret their point and purpose. Despite these possibilities, Sangiovanni insists that the practice-dependent approach will generate first principles that will 'vary, at a fundamental level, with respect to the institutional context they are meant to regulate' due to the fact that interpretation 'constrains the content of the principles' (2008: 164). But how does he arrive at this conclusion?

Sangiovanni would have to offer additional conditions for relevant institutional features in order to say anything about the scope of justice from his institutional point of view.

Of course, this does not imply that we cannot limit the scope when theorising justice. This can be done in several ways. It can be done 'directly', for example by following Rawls and focusing on a fixed scope, looking at which principles of justice ought to govern a kind of institution, namely liberal constitutional democracy (Rawls 1993). Or it can be done 'indirectly', for example by following Thomas Nagel and limiting the object of study to a specific kind of institutional relation, in his case between fellow citizens of sovereign states, which in turn motivates (and allegedly justifies) a certain scope (Nagel 2005). However, Sangiovanni neither takes the direct route nor succeeds in the indirect one, since we find actual and institutionally mediated practices globally.

To sum up, our aim in this chapter has been to show that the two most influential arguments for how practices put *political* constraints on normative political principles fail.

NOTES

1. For an overview, see Galston (2010).
2. In our view, however, there is one reasonable interpretation of the ethics first premise, according to which morality has a *justificatory* priority over politics when theorising political legitimacy (see Erman and Möller 2015a). But this alternative is overlooked by realists.
3. Certainly, it remains controversial exactly how little overlap with commonsensical beliefs about what is morally right is compatible with talking about moral rightness, but it is wholly uncontroversial that very little is needed as long as a speaker can be interpreted as expressing beliefs about what to do. Some theorists, such as Richard Hare (1952) and Allan Gibbard (2003), argue that there are no naturalistic constraints at all. Others, such as Philippa Foot (1959) and Frank Jackson and Philip Pettit (1995) think there needs to be *some* overlap with substantial moral beliefs held by others in the community.
4. The analysis of thick concepts is highly controversial, but this is the fundamental feature most theorists agree upon. For classical accounts of thick concepts, see McDowell (1978, 1979) and Williams (1985). For contemporary analyses, see Dancy (2004); Eklund (2011); and Väyrynen (2013).
5. Compare with the discussion in the previous section.

6. Approaches that take into account interpretations of existing practices in their reasoning about justice have often been accused of a kind of 'status quo bias'. For example, many have argued that this is a problem in Rawls' domestic theory of justice (see, for example, Barry 1995; Goodin 1998; Gibbard 1991). It might be the case that this criticism could also be directed at the institutional version of practice-dependence treated here. However, the problem of the status quo will not be of immediate interest in this section.

7. While Ronzoni also agrees that the appropriate principles of justice for *specific* existing practices depend on the nature of those very practices, the establishment of new practices are seen as derivatively justified under circumstances when this is the only way of preserving the justice of practices that already exist (Ronzoni 2009: 231).

8. So that while it is true in *Nineteen Eighty-Four* that Winston Smith lives in Oceania, it could not be true that Oceania is unjust.

9. The counterfactual force of reflective equilibrium is exactly what David Brink utilises for the semantics of moral terms in general (Brink 2001).

Chapter 7

STALEMATES AND WAYS FORWARD

═══════════

In the individual chapters, we have tried to demonstrate how practice-based theorists in the debates analysed have drawn erroneous or overly strong conclusions about how social and political practices in different ways constrain normative political principles. In our view, this has led to all five debates reaching an impasse with regard to answering the overall research question of this book, namely what role social and political practices should play in the justification of normative political principles. In this chapter, we begin by addressing three general misunderstandings revealed by our analysis, which have contributed to this deadlock. Our overall conclusion is that the main fault of the practice-based view is that it understands the relationship between practices and principles in terms that are too one-directional and static. Thereafter, we argue that as soon as we clear up these three misunderstandings, a much more flexible view of the relationship between practices and principles comes to the fore. More specifically, we defend two constraints on normative political principles: what we call the 'fitness constraint' and the 'functional constraint'. The fitness constraint is a requirement on the relationship among the commitments made in an account, whereas the functional constraint is an explicitly context-dependent requirement due to the role the account is intended to play in normative political theory.

THREE GENERAL MISUNDERSTANDINGS

The theorists treated in this book constitute a heterogeneous group, working within different subdomains of political theory. A substantial aim of the book has been to show that despite their differences, they not only address the same fundamental question of how social and political practices relate to normative political principles, but also share the assumption that practices in different ways *constrain* principles. Our analysis so far has demonstrated, in some detail, particular overextensions and faulty claims that these practice-based theorists have taken to be motivated by their concern for not losing sight of the actual practice to which a principle is to be applied. In this section, we will suggest three overarching misunderstandings that our analysis of the practice-based view discloses, which have to do with justificatory direction, ontological and epistemological aspects, and feasibility constraints in normative theorising. We address each under separate headings below.

Justificatory Direction

Recall that the practice-based method includes, first, the meta-norm that the content and justification of a normative political principle is dependent on the nature of the practice it is intended to govern, and second, the three-step interpretive methodology (James 2005, 2012; Sangiovanni 2008; Ronzoni 2009, 2011; Rossi 2012). As we saw with regard to the interpretive strategy for defending the stronger 'distinct' reading of this method, proponents utilise the conceptual distinction between *interpretation* and *application* to chisel out the particular constraints on normative political principles that the practice-based method entails. In light of our analysis in Chapter 4, we infer that there is a more general problem with this strong reading of the practice-based method, which comes in the form of a logical fallacy. To illustrate this, let us formulate in two general propositions the core premises of mainstream (practice-independent) and practised-based approaches as they are depicted by supporters of the practice-based method:

> (PI) Basic (moral) principles P justify a first principle of justice, J, which when applied in various contexts $(C_1–C_n)$ justifies the applied principles $J_{c1}–J_{cn}$.

> (PB) A first principle of justice, J, is justified by an interpretive understanding of the practices that the principle is intended to govern.

We argue that advocates of the practice-based method make the logical fallacy of taking the truth of a conditional to also imply the denial of its converse; in this case, to wrongly believe that the proposition 'p justifies q' precludes the endorsement of the proposition 'q justifies p'. If we take a closer look at (PI) and (PB), they both endorse justification in *one* direction, but, significantly, neither account prohibits justification in the *reverse* direction. Consequently, if we could endorse the possibility that two propositions can give each other support, rather than the justification going only in one direction, there are no necessary constraints on normative political principles following from the practice-based method. And, as we saw in Chapter 4, this holistic method of justification (reflective equilibrium) is typically endorsed by practice-based and mainstream theorists alike.

Hence, it is misleading to depict the distinction between interpretation and application in terms of 'bottom-up' and 'top-down' approaches, as is often done by practice-based theorists. On this picture, practised-based theorists adopt a bottom-up approach according to which a normative political principle is justified from *below* through interpreting relevant practices, whilst mainstream theorists adopt a top-down approach according to which a normative political principle is justified from *above* by applying a more general moral principle. However, as soon as we avoid the logical fallacy above and instead endorse the idea that the justificatory direction is a two-way rather than a one-way affair, we gain a much more reasonable picture of justification. Acknowledging that the propositions (PI) and (PB) can give each other support, the theorist may conceive of her theory through reflecting and abstracting from specific cases, and she may also investigate how general principles should apply to specific cases. As we have stressed by looking at the process of reflective equilibrium, the theorist is obliged to make her account as consistent as possible. But neither the practice-based theorist nor the mainstream theorist is (or rather should be) committed to an exclusive justificatory direction: both top-down and bottom-up justificatory relations are permitted.

Importantly, we must avoid the misconception, which the term 'application' may fool us into forming, that the mainstream theorist is committed to some sort of 'deductive' justificatory scheme. That would be a grave mistake. No mainstream theorist believes that we may, even in principle, *deduce* our normative political principles from an algorithmic application of some set of general moral principles. Even the archetypical practice-independent and moralist theorist, Cohen, explicitly points out that his account does not entail that we deduce applied principles from general ones (Cohen 2003: 220). Application always requires judgement and interpretation. As we noted in Chapter 3, actual states of affairs are descriptively open-ended, and general principles are typically underspecified (what does it mean exactly, for example, that we should respect all people equally?), so whether a principle applies to a context will in general not be a matter of deduction. Mainstream theorists have always stressed that the application of normative principles requires judgements, assessments and possible trade-offs against the backdrop of a specific context in which the action is supposed to take place.

Ontological and Epistemological Aspects

The second misunderstanding revealed through our overall analysis of the practice-based view concerns the difference between ontological and epistemological aspects. As we have seen in previous chapters, practice-based theorists agree that we must carefully interpret the nature of the practice that the intended normative political principle is supposed to govern. And understanding its nature, as discussed in Chapter 5, includes both an objective and a subjective component: the objective component consists of knowledge of the point and purpose of the practice, the values guiding the practice as well as the structure of the interactions among the participants; the subjective component consists of knowledge of the underlying or motivating values and self-understandings of the participants as well as their reasons for supporting and sustaining the practice.

We have already shown in Chapter 5 that the stronger demand made by practice-based theorists is implausible. Here, we want to extend our criticism with the claim that this stronger demand for knowing about the nature of a practice and the reasoning of its participants emerges from a conflation of ontology with epistemology. The idea that we need such knowledge in order to theorise proper normative political principles goes well beyond the uncontroversial demand made by mainstream theorists that information about existing institutional and political contexts is required in coming to a concrete judgement about which regulatory rule or course of action is the best possible way forward from where we are now (Sangiovanni 2016: 3). Moreover, it represents a specifically *epistemological* demand. But from what does this demand originate? Certainly, many practice-based theorists have been heavily influenced by John Rawls' constraining condition on principles, according to which 'the correct regulative principle for anything depends on the nature of each thing' (Rawls 1971: 29). But such nature-dependence seems to entail at most that a principle must be *applicable* to a practice, or that it is *compatible* with that practice. As expressed by Charles Beitz: since regulative principles are supposed to regulate the conduct and structure of a practice, any candidate principle for this practice must be 'formulated in such a way that it satisfies a condition of applicability' (Beitz 2014: 227).

Consider Sangiovanni's often-used example of the EU as the target practice. There seems to be one piece of information that is necessary for every normative account of the EU: that the suggested normative political principle may count as a principle *for* the EU. In order for a principle to count as a principle for the EU, the practices for which it may be a guiding principle must be compatible with the EU. Hence, if what is required for abiding by the principle is a world government, it may reasonably be objected that this principle cannot be a principle for the EU, since a world government is beyond the scope of the EU. Or consider football and imagine a football league for which we wonder which principles of justice should guide the matches. Suppose the players argued that the most just way of determining who wins would be through lottery, regardless of the actual score, since it would be unjust that different talents and skill sets decided the outcome as they are not deserved but came about through the natural lottery (nature and nurture). In such a case, it may be objected that this principle of justice may not be a principle of justice for the football league, since it would go against the nature of football, where the score settles the matches, no matter how unjust that score may be (and often is, at least according to the supporters of the losing team).

What has been utilised in these examples, however, is only that a principle must be compatible with, or applicable to, a practice. And this is an *ontological* constraint, having to do with how things *are* as a matter of fact, and does not entail any particular epistemological constraint, having to do with what we *know*, for example about the implicit understandings of the point and purpose of the practice or the participants' motivating values. Such epistemological requirements go well beyond the ontological applicability constraint.

Below, we will show that keeping these ontological and epistemological issues apart opens up space for a much wider variance in scope for constraints than acknowledged by practice-based theorists: sometimes the constraints are demanding; other times there are practically no constraints at all at play.

Feasibility Constraints in Normative Theorising

In relation to all suggested constraints treated in previous chapters, a third misunderstanding found in the literature concerns the view of feasibility constraints in normative theorising. As discussed in Chapter 2, the motivating force behind the emergence of the practice-based view in the debates reviewed is a dissatisfaction with what mainstream theory has had to offer in terms of action-guidance and practical import, since their abstract higher-level principles are often not feasible even in the very remote future. However, it seems to be a grave mistake to categorically dismiss certain theories on the basis of feasibility in this way if we want to answer the question of what role practices play in the formulation and justification of normative principles. Above all, this dismissal seems to rely on a view of feasibility constraints in binary terms, such that ideal and non-ideal theory are seen as two *kinds* of theory that cannot be pursued simultaneously.

Such a binary understanding overlooks that it is the *relationship* between principles that matters when assessing the soundness of an account. If we instead see feasibility constraints in terms of a continuum, we open up for a more full-fledged analysis of how practices may delimit principles. On this view, the theorist may adopt different feasibility constraints depending on what work the intended principle is supposed to do in relation to the problem at hand. So, for example, if we ask the question of what principles of justice should regulate our own university now and in the near future, we would presumably work under more demanding feasibility constraints then if we ask what a fully just world would look like. At the same time, when theorising concrete and context-bound principles of the former kind, we should not ban certain kinds of principles because they are too abstract and ideal. Instead, it is the relationship between the candidate principles that is important. In the present case, this means that we have to investigate the relationship between the principles of justice for our university and the principles of justice for the fully just world. The requirement for a plausible account is that in answering the question of what a fully just world requires, say, under the feasibility constraint that it must be physically possible to achieve for humans from our current situation, the principles we come up with must be compatible with the principles we defend for our university, say, under the feasibility constraint that they must be realisable within the near future using the university's current resources; if they are not, at least one of them has to be reformulated or abandoned. What we mean by compatible here is that the more applied principles must also be defendable from the standpoint of the more fundamental principles *in view of* the more demanding feasibility constraints, and vice versa (more on this below).

Our overall conclusion, from analysing the current theoretical literature with regard to how social and political practices condition normative political principles, is that the relationship between practices and principles is understood in terms that are too fixed and one-directional to appropriately answer this question. As we will argue next, as soon as we avoid the above misunderstandings and instead acknowledge a two-way justificatory direction, carefully separate ontological and epistemological aspects, as well as see feasibility constraints as a continuum rather than in binary terms, a flexible approach presents itself, which allows much more normative freedom for the theorist.

WHAT CONSTRAINTS ON PRINCIPLES ARE DEFENSIBLE?

Probably coming as no surprise for the reader, we think that due to the many potential – and perfectly respectable – aims in political theory there is little in the way of a pre-set list of constraints for the normative theorist. The theorist has, we firmly believe, substantial freedom and flexibility in developing her theory, which should be judged on its own merits. Whether it falls short or is successful depends on the exact context of the case rather than some pre-set context of politics to which it must conform.

What does this mean, in more detail? Well, at the very least it means that there are less constraints on political theorising than have been argued for by the theorists criticised in this book. But our 'bold conjecture' goes well beyond this. Indeed, we find it reasonable to take the informed stance that there is *no* set of substantive methodological or justificatory constraints that the theorist attempting to justify a normative political principle in political theory needs to adhere to. In the book, we have discussed – and criticised – many such constraints, and found them to be unsubstantiated. Taking practices, the foul play of actual political agents or any such (supposedly) factual circumstances *into consideration* means no more, and no less, than including them in the justificatory equation. Maybe they have justificatory traction; but then again, maybe not. It is all part of the justificatory process: whether they do is something in need of an argument. Consequently, arguing that we *must* look closely at this or that part of the empirical world becomes, we think, either trivial or illegitimate. It becomes trivial if interpreted in terms that are already normative, such as 'all relevant empirical circumstances should be taken into consideration', since the question of what should count as relevant is itself part of a normative argument. It becomes illegitimate if some substantive set of empirical circumstances is singled out as justificatory delimiting at the outset (for example, that the account must correspond to current properties of politics, such as disagreement or self-interest), for the same reason: what is normatively relevant is a first-order question, part of the normative argument, not a precondition for the theorist.

Of course, the truth of our conjecture will depend on what counts as 'substantive'. We know of no good way to directly spell that out any clearer than in variants of the claim of the last paragraph, that is, in terms of the primacy of the normative argument itself. In general, substantive constraints are the *product* of the normative argument, not its premise. That said, we believe that a clearer picture of what we have in mind may be reached through two steps.

The first step has already been taken. In the book, we have given plenty of examples of false, or at least unjustified, constraints, both normative and empirical. When we talk about 'substantive constraints', we have constraints of those kinds in mind, which attempt to delimit the normative space at the outset, regardless of the intended aim of the theorists.

The second step, to which we now turn, is to say something about the constraints we do take there to be on normative theorising. In this section, we will develop our thoughts and locate them in our overall picture. We will focus on two kinds of constraints, which we call the 'fitness constraint' and the 'functional constraint'.

THE FITNESS CONSTRAINT

On our construal, the remedy to the justificatory direction fallacy of practice-based theorists, discussed in the previous section, is to endorse a holistic attitude toward justification, focusing instead on avoiding incoherence and ensuring that proper supporting relations are in place in the account – whether or not that support comes from a strong belief in a fundamental (typically moral) principle or several sources with less than full independent justification – which taken together support the

conclusion sought. In terms of constraints on theories, the overly con-
servative one-directional justification should thus be replaced with a
so-called 'fitness constraint'.

The fitness constraint, in its most abstract form, is the idea that the
normative political principle argued for in a theorist's account should
fit together with the other principles, values and states of affairs which
are (or should be) endorsed in the account.[1] If a suggested principle
of justice does not fit together with the fundamental moral principles
and values subscribed to in the account, or with other political principles or values endorsed, the account is justificatory deficient. If, on the
other hand, the endorsed principles, values and particular claims in the
account fit well with each other, the suggested principle of the account
is justificatory strengthened.

The fitness constraint thus requires that the set of commitments of
the account is in harmony. And rather than the rigid constraint envisioned by practice-based theorists, where justification has a set direction, the fitness constraint puts a *dynamic* condition on the principle
that the account sets out to justify. Any direction of justification, whether
bottom up or top down, or a set of commitments on an equal level of
prior justificatory force, is allowed. This is the case because the conditions of fitness concern the ways in which *all* relevant claims fit together
in the account. Simply put, in order for the account to be justified, it
must fit with the other claims on which the account is premised. If there
appears to be tensions between different commitments of the account,
regardless of other virtues, they must be resolved before the account
may be considered justified. And the resolution may only be made in
either of two fundamental ways (or a combination): by abandoning at
least one of the commitments in the account, or by showing that there
actually is no tension after all.

The fitness constraint, as we envision it, has a negative and a positive aspect. The negative aspect of the fitness constraint is its purely
'threshold' function, which may be explicated in terms of consistency.
In order for an account to be valid, the set of commitments it contains (explicitly or implicitly) must be *consistent* with each other. In the
weakest sense, this could mean logical consistency, but that is arguably setting the bar a little too low: that slavery should be permitted
and that it should be forbidden to own another person is not logically
inconsistent, but we typically take it to be inconsistent in the sense
sought. Hence, something closer to analytic or conceptual consistency
seems to be the minimal threshold: if slavery entails the ownership of

another person, the two normative claims are obviously inconsistent. But it seems to us that less formal senses of consistency may also come into play here: claiming that slavery should be banned but that you should be permitted to lease people for a contracted amount of time is perhaps not analytically inconsistent. Still, the two claims seem to be in internal tension and thus demand an explanation for how they both may hold.

The positive aspect of the fitness constraint is about justificatory force. Whereas the negative aspect is binary in that it supplies a threshold over which a potentially valid account must pass, the positive aspect is a matter of degree: the stronger support the suggested principle is given by the other premises and claims of the account, the more justified it is.[2] That a principle of, say, equality, is *compatible* with the equal value of all, naturally provides less justification of a principle of equality than if the equal value of all bears a more directly supporting relation, such that the latter *explains* the soundness of the principle, or perhaps even (although the term suggests more empirical data) provides *evidence* for the principle. In line with our basic stance of normative freedom, we suggest that the question of which relations between commitments do in fact provide a supporting function, and to which degree they do so, is a *substantial* matter to be argued for in the actual account rather than considered to be pre-theoretically settled. That said, we will outline the most common examples of supportive relations between particular commitments as well as within the set of commitments as a whole in the section 'The Justificatory Freedom of Fitness' below. First, however, let us address the affinity between the fitness constraint and reflective equilibrium.

Fitness and Reflective Equilibrium

Fitness, as we have envisioned it, bears a close resemblance to coherence accounts in epistemology.[3] This is not a coincidence; in particular, we take the fitness constraint to be in accordance with the most famous of all methods[4] in political philosophy: the method of reflective equilibrium (Rawls 1951, 1999), which we discussed primarily in Chapter 4. As we may recall, on the method of reflective equilibrium, the aim is to find a stable point where our basic normative intuitions (our 'considered moral judgements') and our general principles harmonise or hang together. The idea is to reach a state in which all of the normative commitments we hold are in harmony with our general principles and norms. Reflective equilibrium is thus a state of balance across all levels of generality of our norms.

Most likely, achieving (or more likely approaching)[5] this state means that we have to abandon some of our specific normative intuitions, since they would not fit with other intuitions or principles. Importantly, however, this is true of our principles too: if we find that on closer examination they go against normative intuitions that we are simply not prepared to abandon, the principles must be modified. The method of reflective equilibrium does not favour one set of intuitions or principles as more fundamental than any other. Which principles, norms or particular normative judgements that survive the process is an open question which will depend on the prior conviction the agent holds in relation to her beliefs as well as with how each belief coheres with the rest of the set. In principle, as far as the method is concerned, no judgement or principle is immune to revision.

We think that the properties just stated make reflective equilibrium a good candidate for explicating the fitness constraint. This is interesting in the current context, since despite the fact that many of the theorists treated in this book insist on constraints that are both stronger and in tension with the process of reflective equilibrium, at least in the minimum sense discussed here, this process is endorsed by virtually all theorists in political theory, practice-based as well as more mainstream ones. That said, reflective equilibrium has had its share of critics over the years, and in order to explain further what we take the fitness constraint to include (and what it does not include), we will now touch upon some of these issues.

Fitness and Ultimate Justification

One critique of coherence accounts of justification in general and reflective equilibrium in particular relates to the concern that mere fitness between beliefs is compatible with having false beliefs: especially if the 'net' of beliefs which are internally coherent is local enough. According to these critics, unless we have some subset of 'fundamental' beliefs which are justified in ways other than through their fit with other beliefs, our beliefs are not justified. Coherentists, on the other hand, argue that there is no bedrock of beliefs which are justified in themselves. This 'myth of the given', which Wilfrid Sellars criticised in his seminal *Empiricism and the Philosophy of Mind* (Sellars 1997) is based on a wish for something that simply is not there. As Wittgenstein puts it: 'If I have exhausted the justifications I have reached bedrock, and my spade is turned. Then I am inclined to say: "This is simply what I do"' (1953: §217).

While we are inclined to side with the anti-foundationalist camp when it comes to the very idea of 'ultimate justification', our fitness constraint, as we interpret it, is orthogonal to both foundationalism and coherentism as full-blown theories of justification. As we see it, the fitness constraint is a coherence condition which applies to *either* theory, that is, whether or not you believe there to be any such thing as a set of beliefs that are self-justified. The coherentist should have no problem with anything that is said so far, obviously. But even for the foundationalist's account to be justified, her set of claims needs to be internally coherent. If not, either what she took to be self-evident (or otherwise self-justified) is in fact false, or (perhaps more probable) some of the other claims need to go. This is not to say, of course, that the foundationalist or the coherentist would not have *additional* demands on justification; they typically do. Our point here is merely that both camps must reasonably acknowledge the constraint on their theories that all commitments they make fit together.

So far our compatibility-point is this: the fitness constraint is in line with both coherentism and foundationalism in epistemology. Moreover, we suggest that further concerns of full-blown epistemological theories are either orthogonal to political theory or part of a substantial argument. Hence, they cannot be used to 'disqualify' an entire class of normative theories. Answers to questions concerning the existence of ultimately justified belief, whether or not the 'circles' of coherence between our beliefs need to be large or small, or exactly what it means that a claim fits with another claim, are either irrelevant for normative political theory or part and parcel of the very critique of a *particular* theory (as opposed to a critique of 'mainstream political theory' as a kind of theory, as expressed by practice-based theorists).

The question of foundational justification is typically irrelevant, we suggest, since the principles and premises in political theory that we are interested in are bad candidates for bedrock entities in any case. We cannot think of any interesting, and thus substantial, claims in political theory which are not to some extent controversial and whose justification is fully certain. That goes for normative principles and values (such as the equal value of all persons) as well as descriptive claims (such as claims about the nature of human beings). What this means is that demonstrating that they are justified must be either part of the account, or simply assumptions on which the account hinges. Likewise, criticism of the account should come as an actual counter-argument of the thesis in question rather than as a set of substantial pre-theoretical constraints. So, for example, the theorist who opposes Cohen's account of justice, rather than attempting to put an epistemological or a methodological ban on his foundationalist theory of justification (rational intuitionism), should engage with what Cohen takes to be the upshot of his intuitionism, that is, the very fundamental principles he bases his account on, or the argument he infers from these basic premises (Cohen 2003, 2008). All theorists come to the table with a set of beliefs, normative or descriptive, which they take to be justified. The critic should focus on meeting the substantial arguments for them rather than complaining that, say, there are no infallible intuitions in ethics and politics. For example, as we have shown in Chapter 6, a constraint such as 'never assume, in your theory, that people may agree' is something that needs to be argued for in the very context of the target account, not least since the aim of a political theory is not unitary.

The Justificatory Freedom of Fitness

In accordance with our basic suggestion made in Chapters 3 and 6 that the proper level for debating the pros and cons of normative accounts in political theory is on the level of *first-order* theorising (rather than on the metatheoretical level), we take the 'fitness' in the fitness constraint to be ironed out in the actual account – or to be criticised given the details of the account. What we mean by this is that rather than attempting to develop theoretical constraints on what kinds of justifications are proper, the theorist should engage with the justificatory structure sought in the case at hand. If the theorist is developing an account, she should focus on the (sufficiently hard) task of motivating her premises and developing the argument for the normative principle she advocates. Likewise, if she is criticising a rival account, she should focus on finding flaws in what she takes to be the best arguments for it.[6]

Such flaws may, naturally, include justificatory objections. But due to the multitude of potential justificatory strategies, and the dependence of these strategies on the context of the account (including its aim), we should refrain from pre-theoretically attempting to ban one strategy or the other, as a matter of principle. Sometimes we are right in claiming that the availability of a match may justify the inference that we will be able to light the fire. In other, less ideal circumstances, we are not. If the wood is wet, or we are up in space where there is no oxygen, we are not justified in concluding that the fire will light.

What this amounts to in terms of the fitness constraint, is what we could call justificatory freedom. Rather than pre-determined justificatory constraints on what counts as 'fitting', we set no such constraints at all. The theorist may thus start with a set of premises she takes to be fundamental in some relevant sense and infer from them the conclusion sought. As we have seen examples of in this book, such one-directional justificatory paths may be either 'top down' or 'bottom up'. In the former case, they may start with a set of abstract principles which the theorist takes to have strong (independent) justification, and from there argue for a more concrete or applied principle. In the latter case, they may start with a set of applied principles or particular normative judgements (which, similarly, the theorist takes to be strongly supported at the outset), and from there argue that a more abstract principle holds. Both of these one-directional justificatory paths may succeed, and should thus not be prohibited from the start.

Alternatively, we may have no set of principles or propositions in which we have optimal confidence, but instead rely for our justification on the particular way in which these principles and other propositions fit together. We then rely on the coherence of (a relevant subset of) our entire belief system. As mentioned above, such coherence is no guarantee for truth; but whether or not it provides sufficient support will depend on the exact way in which our propositions hang together, and what degree of independent reliance we place on them. In other words, it will depend on the details of the case at hand.

Famously, in order to respond to the charge that coherentist theories of justification do not track truth, Rawls and other advocates of reflective equilibrium have stressed the difference between wide and narrow reflective equilibrium (Rawls 1974). Narrow reflective equilibrium is when all of our normative beliefs – considered judgements and general principles and values – fit together, more or less regardless of which set of propositions we have taken under consideration. Wide reflective equilibrium, on the other hand, demands that we consider a much broader set of different alternatives and thoughts, in particular the philosophical arguments and theories which are relevant for the case at hand. While in his early writings, it was not clear whether Rawls' account of reflective equilibrium was of the narrow or the wide kind, Rawls later stressed (Rawls 1974), and other theorists concurred (e.g. Daniels 1979) that wide reflective equilibrium was the relevant notion for moral theory.

The main reason for preferring wide to narrow reflective equilibrium is of course that while any random set of beliefs may cohere without being the least plausible from an external viewpoint, taking the best viable philosophical arguments into consideration means that the theorist cannot simply turn a blind eye to good arguments. The theorist would thus at the very least be informed by the current standing in philosophy, hopefully insulating the account from utilising implausible premises and arguments.

We agree that wide reflective equilibrium is preferable to a narrow equilibrium, but still want to stress that we perceive the fitness constraint as a formal, non-substantial constraint. And as such, it is neutral (or silent) as to the substance of the propositions taken under consideration – as long, that is, as they fit together. That an account has not considered a good philosophical argument against some of its premises or inferences is indeed a flaw. And in some cases, an account cannot reasonably be said to be justified unless some reasonable objections to it have been considered. But we take these concerns – again – to be a matter of the actual, first order argumentations for or against an account, and not part of any pre-determined constraints on an account. Although perhaps not plausible, it is at least conceivable that the most convincing theory of justice ever to be developed 'slices the bread' in a completely new way, that is, argues for the normative account of justice from a perspective no one has ever thought about before. While that account would have to fulfil the fitness constraint, it would not necessarily be in wide reflective equilibrium. This is one way in which our fitness constraint, while in strong affinity with reflective equilibrium, is distinct from it.

Another point of debate of relevance for the justificatory freedom of the fitness constraint is to what extent, if any, there are *external* rather than *internal* reasons. On an internal reason construal, the only legitimate reasons (or the only entities that really count as a reason) are internal reasons, which typically refer to something along the lines of 'considerations which motivate the agent in question'.[7] On such a view, normative justification is importantly agent-relative, and the question of what the theorist *should* endorse becomes a question of what the theorist *does* endorse given some actual or counterfactual circumstances. A theorist advocating, say, slavery, may do so based on values according to which some people are less worthy than others, or perhaps that the 'right' to self-ownership is a commodity rather than a basic human right. If the considerations brought forward, by the theorist herself or by others, manage to either change her endorsement of these values, or the way in which they contribute to her overall advocacy of slavery, the case against slavery is successful.

On an external reason construal, a reason is a consideration which speaks in favour of a conclusion, where the speaking-in-favour relation bears no necessary relation to the motivation of the agent. On such a view, a consideration may be a reason for an agent to reject, for example, slavery, even if the consideration is not endorsed by the agent. Hence, the consideration that all people have equal worth may be a reason against slavery for the person who also believes that some have lesser value than others.

We wholeheartedly endorse external reasons. The sadist also has a reason against torturing an innocent child, such as that it would hurt it and be against its volition, even if the sadist is not motivated by these considerations. But, again, we think that such metatheoretical concerns should not be part of any constraint on normative theory as such. If the account of a theorist is premised on the idea that torturing innocent children is *good* regardless of what anyone thinks, as long as whatever else she endorses fits with this premise, the fitness constraint does not reject the account, either on the basis that it contains an assumption that reasons are external or that its assumption is morally problematic. Indeed, we think that both of these potential objections should be tested in substantial first-order deliberation. Consequently, on our view defended here, the question of whether a society should reject slavery or torture even in cases where their citizens believe both practices to be sound, becomes yet another first-order normative question. Not, that is, a constraint on an account as such.

Is the Fitness Constraint a Methodological Constraint?

The close affinity between our interpretation of the fitness constraint and what is commonly called the method of reflective equilibrium raises the question of whether the fitness constraint is correctly viewed as a *methodological* constraint. As we see it, the answer to this question is in the negative: the fitness constraint is compatible with virtually any methodology, that is, it is a condition on an account regardless of the methodology utilised by the theorist. But since the answer to the question depends on what counts as a methodological constraint, and the idea that some methods are obligatory is commonplace among practice-based theorists, let us explain what we mean in more detail.

As is now familiar, the fitness constraint requires that the commitments of the normative political account in question fit with each other in a holistic manner. Typically, in order to fulfil this requirement, the theorist starting to formulate and develop a normative account in political theory would have to engage in processes of introspection and modification of the set of commitments she takes to be part of the account. Such a process would typically consist of comparing the specific normative commitments about particular instances, principles and values, and revising these when there is a lack of fit between them. Such a revision would typically be guided by the strength of the theorist's particular commitments – for example, which of them she is most unwilling to give up and which can more easily be 'sacrificed' for reaching a coherent whole – as well as the theoretical commitments about justified belief revision, in order to achieve a sufficient level of coherence between all of the commitments of the account. Finally, if the theorist is successful, her account fulfils the fitness constraint.

Now, we do not deny that it makes sense to call this process a 'method'. Indeed, we take it that Rawls and other theorists refer to 'the method of reflective equilibrium' for exactly this reason. For Rawls, it was an explicit aim to describe a proper way of reasoning in the moral and political sphere (Rawls 1951, 1971), and both followers and critics typically think of reflective equilibrium as a method. Still, at least in the case of the fitness constraint,[8] it is strictly speaking false as well as misleading to call it a method. This is so because it is perfectly conceivable, if not entirely probable, that the theorist just happens to formulate an account which at the stage of initial formulation already fulfils the fitness constraint, without the theorists utilising the process outlined above. And in any case, we think it is misleading in the present circumstances to call such a process of belief revision a 'method', since it implies something much 'thicker' and more substantive than the formal requirement that the fitness constraint sets out to be.

Normative and Non-normative Commitments

Let us wind up our analysis of the fitness constraint by discussing how it relates to non-normative commitments. Normative commitments come in many forms (at least when interpreted as broadly as is common in political theory): principles, values, norms and particular normative judgements. The fitness constraint requires all of these commitments to cohere. But the scope of the fitness constraint does not cover only normative commitments. While intentionally carrying little substantive (as opposed to formal or technical) significance, the fitness constraint holds for *all* kinds of claims or commitments: both normative and non-normative commitments must cohere.

Mainstream political theory tends to focus on the normative side of things. This is especially true of post-Rawlsian theory, which typically follows Rawls' emphasis on normative propositions: abstract principles on one extreme, and specific normative intuitions ('considered judgements') on the other. But while this 'fit' is indeed central, the indirect role of non-normative propositions is likewise important. Indeed, a central theme of the present book is about *practices*, and we have repeatedly discussed the role and relevance of non-normative premises (such as full compliance, disagreement, deep conflict and so on) for justifying normative principles.

Non-normative considerations add a dimension of complexity to our overall normative account. First, there is the matter of the *relevance* of a set of non-normative facts for normative theory. One thing practice-based theorists have in common is their emphasis on the constraining role of natural facts, especially facts about human nature. If we ought to do it, we must be able to: ought implies can. But even that is famously controversial. Maybe the truly just society puts demands on us that we cannot live up to. Or more likely, maybe the just society is not psychologically or sociologically stable. In that case, some theorists say 'so much worse for us' (Cohen 2003; Estlund 2014). As we have seen examples of in this volume, this stance is taken to be faulty – indeed on the verge of being insulting (especially for political realists and non-ideal theorists). But even if we grant, as is the more common approach in contemporary political theory, that what we *can* do sets limits for what we *ought* to do, the role of factual consideration is far from clear.

Regardless of our stance in relation to the impossible or highly unlikely, non-normative considerations add complexity to normative political theory in that their relevance is not 'written on their wrist'. They play, in other words, an *indirect* rather than a direct role in normative justification. Famously, in what is commonly called 'Hume's law', a normative conclusion does not follow from a non-normative premise unless a bridge premise is also supplied (Hume 2000).[9] Sometimes, of course, we need not explicitly state the bridge premise. That 'causing pain is *prima facie* bad' is hardly something a theorist needs to argue for in practice. Still, the fit between the different normative claims made in an account of, say, justice, will often depend on implicit bridge premises whose exact nature is left for the reader to figure out for herself. And even when non-normative considerations are brought forward – such as those pertaining to the facts of political life that we discussed in Chapter 6 – it often remains unclear what, more precisely, taking them 'into consideration' amounts to. How does it matter, for example, that it is beyond the scope of an institution to act in accordance with a principle of justice for a society? To considerations such as these we now turn, when discussing our second kind of constraint: the functional constraint.

THE FUNCTIONAL CONSTRAINT

The fitness constraint just outlined is what we take to be the correct alternative to the misconceived 'one-directional' approach to justification mentioned in the first section of this chapter, and to which many practice-based theorists seem to be committed. We now turn to our 'remedy' for the second and third misunderstandings of practice-based theorists, the conflation of ontological and epistemological aspects and the binary understanding of feasibility constraints. Instead of the faulty – and overly strong – constraints originating from these two misunderstandings, we suggest a more modest kind of constraint, which we call the 'functional constraint'. Whereas the fitness constraint represents a formal, non-substantial constraint on normative political accounts, the functional constraint marks out a more substantial requirement on normative political theories. Still, it is explicitly situational, implying little or no substantial limitations to the content of normative political theories *qua* political theories, as opposed to political theories with a certain, more limited function.

Let us explain. By functional constraints, we mean the constraints set on a normative account due to what it aims to *do*, that is, what the suggested principle of the account is supposed to regulate and whether there are any particular limits within which it is intended to do so. The functional constraint involves three key aspects, which, while often being interdependent, can be kept analytically distinct: the principle-kind aspect, the practice-kind aspect and the feasibility aspect.

The Principle-kind Aspect

The principle-kind aspect of the functional constraint emanates from the fact that normative accounts in political theory typically have some sort of limited scope and application in the sense that the suggested principle is a principle of *some kind* for some kind of target practice (the practice-kind aspect is treated below). In normative theory more generally, it is not uncommon to ask the question of what we should do, full stop. Some theorists take accounts of what we are morally obliged to do to supply such an unconstrained normativity: the question of what we should morally do is then the same as the question of what we should do, all things considered.[10] Other theorists take morality to be a more limited domain, and the question of what to do, all things considered, to be a further question even given that we know what is morally right.[11] In political theory, however, the role of our principle is never that unconstrained, but pertains to at least some further specification. When we argue for a principle of justice, we typically do not take it to be conceptually the same as a principle of legitimacy or democracy or fairness. Of course, the question of whether these conceptually distinct principles are extensionally distinct as well is controversial. Some take democracy to be the only legitimate principle of governance, and some take a principle of justice to be a principle of fairness. Others take them to be extensionally distinct, such that a rule may be legitimate even if it is not democratic.

Consequently, in most if not all cases in political theory the principle-kind sought is given in the account, and thus amounts to a substantive restriction on the content of the target principle. If the target principle is a principle of justice, it arguably cannot be a principle which suggests that all goods should be distributed to the person with the biggest feet, or something (we here assume) similarly arbitrary. As we have seen in Chapter 6, political realists make this kind of argument when they – taking their cue from Williams' idea that 'might is not right' (1985) – reason that a legitimate order cannot be based only on power (Rossi and Sleat 2014; Jubb and Rossi 2015; Sleat 2010). The concept of legitimacy is simply not compatible with such an illegitimate order.

In this way, the principle-kind aspect of the functional constraint provides a more substantial constraint on the target principle than the formal fitness constraint discussed earlier. Still, it typically provides a much weaker and less discriminating constraint than practice-based theorists have presumed. As we have argued in Chapter 6 in the case of legitimacy, although not every conceivable political order may reasonably count as legitimate, the counter-argument that an account of legitimacy is not justified on the grounds that it uses a faulty concept of legitimacy typically does not cut very deep. In order to be effective, it must be an argument explaining what is faulty with the notion of legitimacy employed. And such an argument must go well beyond the conceptual domain, because if the only complaint against the account is that it utilises the wrong label for its principle, little has been achieved. As we have stated throughout this book: substantial argument, not semantics, should settle normative debates.

The Practice-kind Aspect

The practice-kind aspect of the functional constraint concerns the ways in which the practice puts functional constraints on the principle. Is the intended principle of justice a principle for the distribution of goods between siblings, the local football team, the nation state, the EU or a world government? Arguably, even if a principle of absolute distributive equality was just, say, within a family, that same principle might not be justified for the EU. Consequently, when developing a normative account, the intended practice plays a central part in shaping the governing principle. A principle for the just appointment of professors at a university, for example, is likely to be different from the just appointment of a leader of a family business. For the former, it makes perfect sense to utilise the Rawlsian idea of positions open to all, with meritocratic concerns playing a major role. For the latter, it is perhaps reasonable to consider family members even when they would not, based on merit, be among the best available candidates, as long as their competence is above a certain threshold.

Indeed, as we have seen throughout the book, the idea that the practice to which the principle applies sets constraints on the principle is essential for practice-based theorists. What we have criticised, however, is not this thought as such, but what these theorists have assumed this to *entail*. As with the constraint emanating from the principle-kind aspect, we must be careful not to overextend the reach of the constraints brought forward by the target practice sought. As we discussed in Chapter 5, the constraints actually set by the intended target practice are less far-reaching than what practice-based theorists have claimed.

One faulty move made by practice-based theorists is what we highlighted as the second misunderstanding of practice-based views, that is, the conflation of epistemological and ontological aspects of a practice. When a theorist is developing a normative account, the intended practice to which it is to be applied surely matters. And at least typically (although we will bring up potential exceptions below), the practice-kind aspect entails that the principle must be compatible with – by which we here mean applicable to – the practice in question. As we have seen, practice-based theorists typically take this to include that we need to investigate the point and purpose of the practice, what reasons its participants have for adhering to it and so on. But, again, such an epistemological requirement does not follow from an onto-logical requirement that the principle must be compatible with (appli-cable to) the practice.

Rather, reasonable epistemological counterparts to an ontological constraint are much weaker. From a requirement that the principle must be compatible with the practice it is intended to regulate, it arguably fol-lows that in order to be *justified*, we should have *good reasons* to think that the suggested principle is applicable to a practice. However, we need not know anything in particular about participants' underlying values and so on to have such good reasons, or have any particular idea about the point and purpose of the practice in question. Exactly what justifica-tion we need arguably varies with the account and practice in question, but usually, what is required is no more than the combination of ana-lytical understanding of the concept in question and knowledge (or at least justified belief) of the empirical circumstances. We typically find out that there is water in the glass, not by wondering about its nature, but by having a reasonable understanding about the concepts 'water' and 'glass', and then actually taste it. And we find out that a principle may be a principle for the EU by investigating whether or not an applica-tion of the principle is compatible with our understanding (conceptual and empirical) of the EU, whether or not this understanding includes an idea about the nature of EU. And for this, the uncontroversial weaker demand of mainstream theory suffices, namely to get information about the relevant context.

Importantly, though, while the requirement that the principle must be compatible with the practice it is intended to regulate is typically a reasonable requirement following from the practice-kind aspect, even this is an open question. We see two cases when the functional con-straint in relation to the intended practice is even weaker.

First, even a principle which is not, strictly speaking, applicable to a practice may *guide* this practice – it may, in other words, be *useful* for a practice even if not compatible with it. In order to motivate this idea, we need only look at models in natural science. A model is merely *similar* in important respects to the phenomenon of interest, and includes some counterfactual assumptions and simplifications which sets it apart from the real phenomenon – indeed, otherwise it would not be a model. But a model of a power plant may still be immensely helpful for, say, the design of a control system for the power plant. Similarly, in the case of politics, it seems to us that the very aim of more or less 'ideal' normative theories is to supply a model case for our actual society. Assuming features that no actual society may ever exemplify – such as full compliance – might be seen exactly as a model of an actual society. Most ideal theorists use such counterfactual devices in order to conceptualise the upper limits for a just or legitimate society.

Indeed, it is easy to find examples of how 'ideal thinking' is utilised in all kinds of areas. A convincing case for how goals which are practically unattainable may serve a useful role is the Vision Zero case in traffic safety. Starting in Sweden in the 1990s, the vision to have *no* causalities in traffic, despite the fact that traffic is *the* most common cause of death for young adults has resulted in a revolutionary rethinking. For example, the main responsibility for traffic safety has shifted from the individual to the system, and the object of safety has shifted from avoiding accidents to avoiding casualties, so that the *severity* of an accident rather than accident prevention per se has come to the forefront. This has resulted in several safety improvements focusing on speed reduction, such as roundabouts, where the number of accidents has increased, but the severity has decreased significantly.[12] Consequently, even ideals which are unattainable may guide action and motivate stakeholders (in this case traffic safety professionals) to act in order to come *closer* to the ideal.

Second, there is always the possibility that when a principle is not compatible with the target practice, *so much the worse for the target practice*. To take an extreme example: if a principle of justice intended to apply to the practice of slavery is in fact not compatible with the practice, modifying the practice – indeed abolishing it in its entirety – seems to be a better way than trying to find a principle of justice which endorses slavery. On a less extreme example, if a principle of justice for the EU would demand, say, a fiscal union, the objection that this would be against the very practice of the EU is not necessarily effective. Rather than defending the idea that a 'fiscal EU' would still be a proper version of the EU, the theorist could concede the category point but withhold that in that case, we should dissolve the EU and form the fiscal union EU_{plus} instead. Consequently, depending on the aim of the normative theorists, the intended practice-kind may entail anything from no constraint at all ('we will redefine the target practice in any way the principle requires') to a very strong, no-modification-possible constraint ('our institution has its brief to which we must stick').

The Feasibility Aspect

As became clear when discussing the variance in strength that the practice-kind puts on a principle, the functional constraint is not always directly captured by what kind of principle it is (the principle-kind aspect) or the kind of practice to which it is to be applied (the practice-kind aspect). To fully explain the functional constraint, we also need to look at the various other aims our principle is intended to fulfil. One central aim, according to practice-based theorists, is captured with the label of 'feasibility', that is, the idea that a principle, in order to be justified, must be feasible, on some relevant interpretation of the term. At the beginning of the chapter, we called the third misunderstanding of practice-based theorists the idea of feasibility understood in *binary* terms, and the corollary that ideal and non-ideal theory are seen as dichotomous, such that they cannot both be pursued. In our view, this picture is erroneous or at least gravely misleading. Instead, we take the reasonable notion of feasibility to be an aspect of the functional constraint. As such, its substantive content is strongly determined by the aim of the normative theorist, by what she is trying to accomplish.

As we have seen in previous chapters, most practice-based theorists claim not only that ideal and non-ideal theory correspond to two dichotomous camps, but that there is something inherently problematic about ideal theory as such. Some even claim that an absence of demanding feasibility constraints automatically makes the account faulty. For example, as we discussed in Chapter 4, Charles Mills criticises theories that utilise concepts and principles which are not based in an actual context for being fundamentally flawed (Mills 2005: 173–5). By not taking present injustices into account (such as structural domination and coercion), and by reflecting the experiences of a small group of people (mostly white middle-class men), these ideal accounts are even dangerous, according to Mills (2005: 167–8, 172). At the other end of the spectrum, some ideal theorists claim that we *must* make use of normative ideals: 'to dive into nonideal theory without an ideal theory in hand is simply to dive blind, to allow irrational free rein to the mere conviction of injustice and to eagerness for change of any sort' (Simmons 2010: 34).

Both claims become unwarranted when we acknowledge the potential difference in function of a normative theory, its aims and goals.[13] Once we take this rather simple idea seriously, the resulting view is a non-binary notion of feasibility, in which there is a continuum of different feasibility constraints we may put on an account. An account may be ideal in comparison with accounts that are construed under more demanding feasibility constraints, and non-ideal in relation to others, which come with more permissive feasibility constraints.[14]

Let us demonstrate with the example of a principle of autonomy. A theorist whose goal is to develop an ideal account of autonomy may assume, for example, that each agent has the material and cognitive means enabling her to pursue a substantial set of potential projects, and argue that autonomy is to be free to choose and to take responsibility for one's life choices. Such an account of autonomy may come with few feasibility constraints, apart from some permissive possibility-constraints, such that the account should be compatible with the basic features of human nature as we know them as well as be possible to achieve with the status quo (Buchanan 2004; Gilabert and Lawford-Smith 2012). Another theorist, who may or may not have formed any determined account of ideal autonomy, is interested in developing an account of autonomy on the domestic level, say, an account of autonomy for children to be applied in the here and now. In such a case, she may take a more demanding set of feasibility constraints to be reasonable. Arguably, paternalistic actions and rules which significantly limit the freedom of choice for the child is plausible for such an account, even if it is not on the idealised account of autonomy.

In this way, many different accounts of autonomy for different agents, groups and practices may be developed, which may (and of course may not) *all* be justified, since they come with different aims, and thus potentially different feasibility constraints. We say 'potentially' however, since, in accordance with our discussion about how a practice may or may not constrain a principle, which, if any, feasibility constraints are reasonable is a *substantial* question, part and parcel of the justification of the account itself. So, while different aims of the theorist might motivate setting limits in terms of, say, how practically action-guiding a principle is, or the plausibility that (most) people would follow the principle, no feasibility constraint is incontestable. And as with the fitness constraint, the contestation should come at the level of first-order theorising, as part of the actual argument for or against an account, not as a pre-determined ban against this or that kind of theory (as in the binary view of feasibility).

The overall picture that we outline here is one in which, in the abstract, there is a multitude of normative accounts with different feasibility constraints, which all may 'co-exist' – which means that they would all be justified (whether they are is another matter). A theorist with the aim of developing a principle of justice for the EU may justify that principle for the very practice it is intended, including arguing for a set of reasonable feasibility constraints given the aim at hand. She may then have no corresponding account of ideal justice, nor any account of justice in the family, or the like. Analogously, another theorist who argues for an account of ideal justice (for example, in the form of an end-state theory) may have little to say about justice in the EU, and a third theorist developing an account of justice in the family may have no account of justice in other domains. In all of these cases, just as in any case of justification, the strength of the account will depend on the substantive arguments given, including the plausibly of the premises used.

That said, *one* way of justifying an account on a particular level of application is to demonstrate how it corresponds to other accounts taken to be plausible. Consequently, by demonstrating that an account of justice in the EU harmonises with a general account of justice, the theorist is demonstrating coherence among accounts on different levels. G. A. Cohen's championed justificatory chain functions exactly in this way. In his famous example, the principle that we should keep our promises is instrumentally justified by being conducive to helping people pursue their projects, where the latter is a more general principle. That principle, in Cohen's example, is ultimately justified by the utilitarian concern that we should promote people's happiness and the premise that only by pursuing their projects can people be happy (Cohen 2003: 216–18). Cohen obviously takes the utilitarian principle to be the only intrinsically justified principle in this example, but that is a further, non-obligatory claim; we may think that keeping promises is intrinsically right, but believe that the fact that it *also* promotes happiness gives us further reason to keep our promises, which may then tip the scale in favour of keeping a promise even in light of other, contrary, concerns.

The upshot here is that while a theorist may keep to a very limited aim of developing an account of, say, justice, for a particular practice in a particular context, she may want to develop accounts on several levels. She may be interested, for example, both in what ideal justice may be *and* the question of how we remove current injustices. Here, we are back to the instigator of the terms ideal versus non-ideal theory: Rawls himself. When Rawls talks about non-ideal theory, he means exactly a theory which deals with the non-ideal circumstances that he 'idealises away' in his ideal account which includes the two principles of justice. The ideal account, on its part, specifies the requisite structural principles and points to 'the overall direction of political action' that must guide the forming of the non-ideal principles (Rawls 1993: 285).

Importantly, though, a theorist who develops principles on different levels in this way, and thus presumes different feasibility constraints, naturally must demonstrate how they fit together; if they do not, something is amiss. Interestingly, this is where our fitness constraint 'meets' our functional constraint: if an account includes an applied principle construed under demanding feasibility constraints and a more general higher-level principle construed under permissive or no feasibility constraints, the applied principle must be reasonable from the standpoint of the higher-level principle *given* the feasibility constraints assumed by the applied principle (and vice versa). This is what the fitness constraint requires.

WINDING UP

In this book, we have analysed five current debates in political theory in search for an answer to the overall question of what role social and political practices should play in the justification of normative political principles. As we have seen examples of throughout the volume, practice-based theorists share the assumption that practices in different ways constrain principles. In our analysis, four kinds of constraints suggested in this literature have been discussed: linguistic constraints, methodological constraints, epistemological constraints and political constraints. We have argued that none of them holds, at least not in the strong way intended. As an alternative, we have proposed two constraints in normative theorising: the fitness constraint and the functional constraint, and have illustrated how they require that both practices and principles be modified under certain circumstances.

An implication of our view is that when the theorist develops her account, she should not at the outset adopt any substantial pre-theoretical constraints, for example, with reference to the function of language or how meaning is construed, to methodological or epistemological assumptions, or to any alleged constitutive features of politics. Instead, she should aspire to fulfil our two suggested constraints, which, as we have seen, allow quite extensive normative freedom in theorising normative political principles in comparison to the practice-based approach.

This normative freedom notwithstanding, our two constraints are also in a sense more demanding than those suggested by practice-based theorists, since they leave much more substantial work to be done by the theorist in developing her account and in criticising others. In our view, it is precisely in the space of giving and asking for reasons that contestations about, for example, the principle-kind, the practice-kind and feasibility constraints should take place and answers be justified through first-order theorising. Insofar as the fitness constraint and the functional constraint are sound, our account also indicates which battles in the debates reviewed are in fact pseudo-battles, where a kind of theory is dismissed due to a failure to abide by some unjustified pre-theoretical constraint, such as ideal theory for not being sufficiently realistic, political moralism for not being sufficiently 'political' or mainstream liberal theory for being too universalistic. As we said in Chapter 1, we believe these debates have involved too many 'ideologically' driven encounters about what is *the* correct way to do normative political theory, which have overshadowed the interesting philosophical puzzles involved in elaborating the relationship between practices and principles. Our hope is that this book, both its critical and its constructive part, has taken at least some steps to push political theory forward by avoiding such dichotomisation and instead proposing reasonable constraints that are generalisable across these five debates, which in our view get to the core of the overall question of what role social and political practices should play in the justification of normative political principles.

NOTES

1. Typically in epistemology, the focus of attention is on the propositional attitude of *belief*. It is the belief of the agent which, in the circumstances the epistemologist attempts to specify, is justified. Here, since we are talking about constraints on normative accounts, we will instead talk about 'claims', 'commitments' and 'endorsements' made by the theorists.
2. The exception here is when the argument is deductive, that is, when the conclusion logically follows from the premises. We have yet to see, however, an argument in the field of political theory which is properly deductive.

3. We have avoided the term here, though, since coherence accounts of justification often contain a denial of any foundationalist accounts of justification. Our fitness account, as will become clear in the section 'Fitness and
Ultimate Justification', takes no stand on the question of ultimate justification and is in this important sense compatible with both coherentist and
foundationalist accounts in epistemology.

4. We will return to the question of whether reflective equilibrium is a method
below.

5. Note that a state of full reflective equilibrium is an ideal state in which it is
highly unlikely that any living being will find herself.

6. Perhaps in most cases, the 'constructive theorist' (the account developer)
and the 'destructive theorist' (the account demolisher) would employ a little
of both: positive arguments for her own preferred account and counter-
arguments for the rival one.

7. There are several versions of reason internalism, and here we only men-
tion the basic version, which may be subjected to various interpretations
(such as whether these considerations are actual or counterfactual, which
generates very different claims). For an excellent overview, see Finlay and
Schroeder 2015.

8. Although we will not press the point here, in line with several commenta-
tors (see, for example, Tersman 1993), we take reflective equilibrium to be
a criterion of rightness for an account or normative theory rather than a
method.

9. Also famously (if not equally so), it is often remarked that it is not at all
clear that Hume himself is committed to this 'law', since what deduction
Hume takes to be 'altogether inconceivable' in the passage of *A Treatise of
Human Nature* where he makes his remarks about 'is' and 'ought' claims is
unclear to say the least (Hume 2000).

10. Richard Hare (1952) famously held such a view, and theorists such as Allan
Gibbard (2003) and Ralph Wedgwood (2001) are contemporary proponents
of this position.

11. Philippa Foot (1959) took morality to be a more substantive kind than
what to do all-things-considered, and among contemporary theorists,
Frank Jackson (1998) argues for the similar idea that there are substantive descriptive conditions which must be in place for us to talk about the
concept of morality.

12. For an overview, see Belin et al. 2012.

13. That said, we believe that non-ideal theorists underestimate the essential
role played by basic values or higher-level principles when they defend
'non-ideal state A' over 'non-ideal state B'. This does not become clear from
the examples often utilised in the literature, such as that we may judge
which of two mountains is higher without knowledge about the highest
mountain in the world, Mount Everest. Such descriptive examples do not

capture what we do when we make normative comparisons. If we consider tallness in relation to jockeys, that is, those who ride horses in horse racing or steeplechase racing, we know that they cannot be too tall because then they will weigh too much (although the famous jockey Lester Piggott was unusually tall, measuring 173 centimetres, hence the nickname 'The Long Fellow'). When we make comparative judgements about the tallness of jockeys, we will use if not a full-fledged ideal theory about optimal height, at least some background values or principles about horse racing.

14. We use this terminology in the main text for its clear imagery, although strictly speaking it is not clear to us that you may order all accounts in relation to their presumed feasibility constraints.

BIBLIOGRAPHY

Abizadeh, Arash (2012), 'On the demos and its kin: nationalism, democracy, and the boundary problem', *American Political Science Review* 104: 867–82.

Archibugi, Daniele (1998), 'Principles of cosmopolitan democracy', in D. Archibugi, D. Held and M. Köhler (eds), *Re-imagining Political Community: Studies in Cosmopolitan Democracy*, London: Polity Press.

Arvan, Marcus (2014), 'First steps toward a nonideal theory of justice', *Ethics & Global Politics* 7(3): 95–117.

Ball, Terence (2010), 'Book review of Talisse's *Democracy and Moral Conflict*', *Notre Dame Philosophical Reviews*.

Banai, Ayelet, Miriam Ronzoni and Christian Schemmel (2011), 'Global social justice: the possibility of social justice beyond states in a world of over-lapping practices', in A. Banai, M. Ronzoni and C. Schemmel (eds), *Social Justice, Global Dynamics: Theoretical and Empirical Perspectives*, Routledge: London, pp. 46–60.

Barry, Brian (1995), *Justice as Impartiality*, Oxford: Clarendon.

Beitz, Charles (2009), *The Idea of Human Rights*, Oxford: Oxford University Press.

Beitz, Charles (2014), 'Internal and external', *Canadian Journal of Philosophy* 44: 225–38.

Belin, Matts-Åke, Per Tillgren and Evert Vedung (2012) 'Vision zero: a road safety policy innovation', *International Journal of Injury Control and Safety Promotion* 19(2): 171–9.

Bellamy, Richard (2010), 'Dirty hands and clean gloves: liberal ideals and real politics', *European Journal of Political Theory* 9: 412–30.

Benhabib, Seyla (2004), *The Rights of Others: Aliens, Residents and Citizens*, Cambridge: Cambridge University Press.

Boonin, David (2008), *The Problem of Punishment*. Cambridge: Cambridge University Press.

Botwinick, Aryeh (1985), *Wittgenstein, Scepticism, and Political Participation: An Essay in the Epistemology of Democratic Theory*, Lanham, MD: University Press of America.

Brandom, Robert (1994), *Making it Explicit*, Cambridge: Cambridge University Press.

Brink, David (2001), 'Realism, naturalism, and moral semantics', *Social Philosophy & Policy* 18: 154–76.

Buchanan, Allen (2002), 'Political legitimacy and democracy', *Ethics* 112: 689–719.

Buchanan, Allen (2004), *Justice, Legitimacy, and Self-Determination*, Oxford: Oxford University Press.

Caney, Simon (2005), *Justice Beyond Borders: A Global Political Theory*, Oxford: Oxford University Press.

Caney, Simon (2006), 'Cosmopolitan justice and institutional design: an egalitarian liberal conception of global justice', *Social Theory and Practice* 32: 725–56.

Carens, Joseph (2000), *Culture, Citizenship, and Community*, Oxford: Oxford University Press.

Christensen, James (2013), 'Practice-dependence, trade, and equality: a review of Aaron James's fairness in practice', *Raisons Politiques* 51(3): 155–66.

Christiano, Thomas (1996), *The Rule of the Many: Fundamental Issues in Democratic Theory*, Boulder, CO: Westview Press.

Christiano, Thomas (2004), 'The authority of democracy', *The Journal of Political Philosophy* 12: 266–90.

Cohen, G. A. (2003), 'Facts and principles', *Philosophy & Public Affairs* 31: 211–45.

Cohen, G. A. (2008), *Rescuing Justice and Equality*, Cambridge, MA: Harvard University Press.

Cohen, G. A. (2009), *Why Not Socialism?*, Princeton, NJ: Princeton University Press.

Dancy, Jonathan (2004), *Ethics without Principles*, Oxford: Clarendon Press.

Daniels, Norman (1979), 'Wide reflective equilibrium and theory acceptance in ethics', *Journal of Philosophy* 76(5): 256–82.

Davidson, Donald (1974), 'On the very idea of a conceptual scheme', *Proceedings and Addresses of the American Philosophical Association* 47: 5–20.

Dryzek, John and Simon Niemeyer (2008), 'Discursive representation', *American Political Science Review* 102: 481–93.

Dworkin, Ronald (1986), *Law's Empire*. Cambridge, MA: Harvard University Press.

Eklund, Matti (2011), 'What are Thick Concepts?', *Canadian Journal of Philosophy* 41: 25–49.

Eldridge, Richard (2003), 'Wittgenstein and the conversation of justice', in C. Heyes (ed.), *The Grammar of Politics: Wittgenstein and Political Philosophy*, London: Cornell.

Erman, Eva (2013), 'In search for democratic agency in deliberative governance', *European Journal of International Relations* 19: 847–68.

Erman, Eva (2014), 'The boundary problem and the ideal of democracy', *Constellations* 21: 535–46.

Erman, Eva and Niklas Möller (2013), 'Three failed charges against ideal theory', *Social Theory and Practice* 39(1): 19–44.

Erman, Eva and Niklas Möller (2014), 'Brandom and political philosophy', *The Journal of Political Philosophy* 22(4): 486–98.

Erman, Eva and Niklas Möller (2015a), 'Political legitimacy in the real normative world: the priority of morality and the autonomy of the political', *British Journal of Political Science* 45(1): 215–33.

Erman, Eva and Niklas Möller (2015b), 'What not to expect from the pragmatic turn in political theory', *European Journal of Political Theory* 14(2): 121–40.

Erman, Eva and Niklas Möller (2015c), 'Practices and principles: on the methodological turn in political theory', *Philosophy Compass* 10(8): 533–46.

Erman, Eva and Niklas Möller (2015d), 'Why political realists should not be afraid of moral values', *Journal of Philosophical Research* 40: 459–64.

Erman, Eva and Niklas Möller (2016a), 'What distinguishes the practice-dependent approach to justice?' *Philosophy & Social Criticism* 42(1): 3–23.

Erman, Eva and Niklas Möller (2016b), 'Why democracy cannot be grounded in epistemic principles', *Social Theory and Practice* 42(3): 449–73.

Erman, Eva and Niklas Möller (2017a), 'How practices do not matter', *Critical Review of International Social and Political Philosophy* (Online First).

Erman, Eva and Niklas Möller (2017b), 'Practice-dependence and epistemic uncertainty', *Journal of Global Ethics* (Online First).

Erman, Eva and Niklas Möller (forthcoming), 'Political legitimacy for our world: where is political realism going?', *The Journal of Politics*.

Estlund, David (2011), 'Human nature and the limits (if any) of political philosophy', *Philosophy & Public Affairs* 39: 207–37.

Estlund, David (2014), 'Utopophobia', *Philosophy and Public Affairs* 42: 113–34.

Farrelly, Colin (2007), 'Justice in ideal theory: a refutation', *Political Studies* 55: 844–64.

Finlay, Stephen and Schroeder, Mark, (2015), 'Reasons for action: internal vs. external', in E. Zalta (ed.), *The Stanford Encyclopedia of Philosophy*, <https://plato.stanford.edu/archives/win2015/entries/reasons-internal-external/≥ (last accessed 2 October 2017).

Foot, Philippa (1959), 'Moral beliefs', *Proceedings of the Aristotelian Society* 59: 83–104.

Forst, Rainer (2011), *The Right to Justification: Elements of a Constructivist Theory of Justice*, trans. J. Flynn, New York: Columbia University Press.

Fossen, Thomas (2013), 'Taking stances, contesting commitments: political legitimacy and the pragmatic turn', *Journal of Political Philosophy* 21: 426–50.

Fossen, Thomas (2014), 'Politicizing Brandom's pragmatism: normativity and the agonal character of social practice', *European Journal of Philosophy* 22: 371–95.

Galston, William (2010), 'Realism in political theory', *European Journal of Political Theory* 9: 385–411.

Gellner, Ernest (1984), 'The gospel according to Ludwig', *The American Scholar* 53: 243–63.

Geuss, Raymond (2008), *Philosophy and Real Politics*, Princeton, NJ: Princeton University Press.

Gibbard, Allan (1991), 'Constructing justice', *Philosophy & Public Affairs* 20: 264–97.

Gibbard, Allan (2003), *Thinking How to Live*, Cambridge, MA: Harvard University Press.

Gilabert, Pablo and Holly Lawford-Smith (2012), 'Political feasibility: a conceptual exploration', *Political Studies* 60: 809–25.

Goodin, Robert (1998), 'What is so special about our fellow countrymen?', *Ethics* 98: 663–86.

Goodin, Robert (2007), 'Enfranchising all affected interests and its alternatives', *Philosophy & Public Affairs* 35: 40–68.

Gowans, Christopher (2000), *Moral Disagreements: Classic and Contemporary Readings*, London: Routledge.

Grönert, Peter (2005), 'Brandom's solution to the objectivity problem', *Pragmatics & Cognition* 13: 161–75.

Gunnell, John (1998), *The Orders of Discourse: Philosophy, Social Science, and Politics*, New York: Rowman and Littlefield.

Gunnell, John (2004), 'Desperately seeking Wittgenstein', *European Journal of Political Theory* 3: 77–98.

Gunnell, John (2013), 'Leaving everything as it is: political inquiry after Wittgenstein', *Contemporary Political Theory* 12: 80–101.

Habermas, Jürgen (1985), 'Questions and counterquestions', in R. Bernstein (ed.), *Habermas and Modernity*, Cambridge, MA: MIT Press.

Habermas, Jürgen (1996), *Between Facts and Norms: Contributions to a Discourse Theory of Law and Democracy*, trans. W. Rehg, Cambridge MA: MIT Press.

Hall, Edward (2017), 'How to do realistic political theory (and why you might want to)', *European Journal of Political Theory* 16: 283–303.

Hare, R. M. (1952), *The Language of Morals*, Oxford: Oxford University Press.

Hooker, Brad (2000), *Ideal Code, Real World: A Rule-consequentialist Theory of Morality*, Oxford: Oxford University Press.

Hooker, Brad and Margaret Little (eds) (2000), *Moral Particularism*, Oxford: Clarendon Press.

Horton, John (2010), 'Realism, liberal moralism and a political theory of modus vivendi', *European Journal of Political Theory* 9: 431–48.

Hume, David (2000). *A Treatise of Human Nature*, ed. D. F Norton and Mary J. Norton, Oxford: Oxford University Press.

Jackson, Frank (1998), *From Ethics to Metaphysics: A Defence of Conceptual Analysis*, Oxford: Oxford University Press.

Jackson, Frank and Philip Pettit (1995), 'Moral functionalism and moral motivation', *The Philosophical Quarterly* 45: 20–40.

James, Aaron (2005), 'Constructing justice for existing practice: Rawls and the status quo,' *Philosophy & Public Affairs* 33: 281–316.

James, Aaron (2012), *Fairness in Practice: A Social Contract for a Global Economy*, Oxford: Oxford University Press.

James, Aaron (2014), 'Reply to critics', *Canadian Journal of Philosophy* 44: 286–304.

Jubb, Robert (2015a), 'The real value of equality', *The Journal of Politics* 77: 679–91.

Jubb, Robert (2015b), 'Playing Kant at the court of King Arthur', *Political Studies* 63: 919–34.

Jubb, Robert (2016), '"Recover it from the facts as we know them"', *Journal of Moral Philosophy* 13: 77–99.

Jubb, Robert and Enzo Rossi (2015), 'Political norms and moral values', *Journal of Philosophical Research* 40: 455–8.

Julius, A. J. (2014), 'Practice-independence', *Canadian Journal of Philosophy* 44: 239–54.

Kant, Immanuel [1793] (1970), 'On the common saying: this may be true in theory, but it does not apply in practice', in H. S. Reiss (ed.), *Kant's Political Writings*, Cambridge: Cambridge University Press.

Lang, Gerald (2001), 'The rule-following considerations and metaethics: some false moves', *European Journal of Philosophy* 9: 190–209.

Lewis, David (1970), 'General semantics', *Synthese* 22: 18–67.

Lister, Andrew (2011), 'Book review of Talisse's *Democracy and Moral Conflict*', *Social Theory and Practice* 37: 363–70.

MacGilvray, Eric (2014), 'Democratic doubts: pragmatism and the epistemic defense of democracy', *Journal of Political Philosophy* 22: 105–23.

Machiavelli, Niccolò [1532] (1961), *The Prince*, trans. G. Bull, London: Penguin.

May, Simon Căbulea (2011), 'Book review of Talisse's *Democracy and Moral Conflict*', *Ethics* 121: 685–90.

McDowell, John (1978), 'Are moral requirements hypothetical imperatives?', *Proceedings of the Aristotelian Society Supplementary* 52: 13–29.

McDowell, John (1979), 'Virtue and reason', *Monist* 62(3): 331–50.

McDowell, John (1984), 'Wittgenstein on following a rule', *Synthese* 58: 325–63.

McDowell, John (1994), *Mind and World*, Cambridge, MA: Harvard University Press.

McGinn, Marie (1997), *Wittgenstein and the Philosophical Investigations*, London: Routledge.

McNaughton, David and Piers Rawling (2000), 'Unprincipled ethics', in B. Hooker and M. Little (eds), *Moral Particularism*, Oxford: Clarendon Press.

Meckled-Garcia, Saladin (2008), 'On the very idea of cosmopolitan justice: constructivism and international agency', *Journal of Political Philosophy* 16: 245–71.

Mill, John Stuart (1859), *On Liberty*, London: The Walter Scott Publishing Co.

Mill, John Stuart (1998), *Utilitarianism*, R. Crisp (ed.), New York: Oxford University Press.

Mills, Charles (2005), '"Ideal theory" as ideology', *Hypatia* 20(3): 165–84.

Misak, Cheryl (2000), *Truth, Morality, Politics: Pragmatism and Deliberation*, New York: Routledge.

Misak, Cheryl (2004), *Truth and the End of Inquiry: A Peircean Account of Truth*, 2nd edition, Oxford: Clarendon Press.

Misak, Cheryl (2008), 'A culture of justification: the pragmatist's epistemic argument for democracy', *Episteme* 5: 94–105.

Misak, Cheryl (2009), 'Truth and democracy: pragmatism and the deliberative virtues', in R. Geenens and R. Tinnevelt (eds), *Does Truth Matter? Democracy and Public Space*, New York: Springer, pp. 29–39.

Misak, Cheryl and Robert Talisse (2014), 'Pragmatist epistemology and democratic theory: a reply to Eric MacGilvray', *Journal of Political Philosophy* 22: 366–76.

Moellendorf, Darrell (2011), 'Why global inequality matters', *Journal of Social Philosophy* 42: 99–109.

Mouffe, Chantal (1999), 'Deliberative democracy or agonistic pluralism?' *Social Research* 66: 745–58.

Mouffe, Chantal (2000), *The Democratic Paradox*, London: Verso.

Mouffe, Chantal (2005), *On the Political*, London: Routledge.

Nagel, Thomas (1991), *Equality and Partiality*, Oxford: Oxford University Press.

Nagel, Thomas (2005), 'The problem of global justice', *Philosophy & Public Affairs* 33: 113–47.

Newey, Glen (2010), 'Two dogmas of liberalism', *European Journal of Political Theory* 9: 449–65.

Norval, Aletta (2006), 'Democratic identification: a Wittgensteinian approach', *Political Theory* 34: 229–55.

Norval, Aletta (2007), *Aversive Democracy: Inheritance and Originality in the Democratic Tradition*, Cambridge: Cambridge University Press.

Norval, Aletta (2009a), 'Democracy, pluralization, and voice', *Ethics & Global Politics* 2: 297–320.

Norval, Aletta (2009b), 'Passionate subjectivity, contestation and acknowledgment', in A. Schaap (ed.), *Law and Agonistic Politics*, Aldershot: Ashgate, pp. 163–78.

Nussbaum, Martha (1986) *The Fragility of Goodness. Luck and Ethics in Greek Tragedy and Philosophy*, Cambridge: Cambridge University Press.

O'Neill, Onora (1987), 'Abstraction, idealization and ideology in ethics', in J. D. G. Evans (ed.), *Moral Philosophy and Contemporary Problems*, Cambridge: Cambridge University Press.

O'Neill, Onora (1996), *Towards Justice and Virtue: A Constructive Account of Practical Reasoning*, Cambridge: Cambridge University Press.

Owen, David (2003), 'Genealogy as perspicuous representation', in C. J. Heyes (ed.), *The Grammar of Politics: Wittgenstein and Political Philosophy*, New York: Cornell University Press.

Philp, Mark (2010), 'What is to be done? Political theory and political realism', *European Journal of Political Theory* 9: 466–84.

Pitkin, Hanna (1972), *Wittgenstein and Justice: On the Significance of Ludwig Wittgenstein for Social and Political Thought*, Berkeley, CA: University of California Press.

Pogge, Thomas (2002), *World Poverty and Human Rights*, Cambridge: Polity Press.

Pohlhaus, Gaile and John Wright (2002), 'Using Wittgenstein critically: a political approach to philosophy', *Political Theory* 30: 800–27.

Rawls, John (1951), 'Outline of a decision procedure for ethics', *Philosophical Review* 60: 177–97.

Rawls, John (1971), *A Theory of Justice*, Cambridge, MA: Harvard University Press.

Rawls, John (1974), 'The independence of moral theory', *Proceedings and Addresses of the American Philosophical Association* 47: 5–22.

Rawls, John (1993), *Political Liberalism*, New York: Columbia University Press.

Rawls, John (1999), 'Kantian constructivism in moral theory', in S. Freeman (ed.), *Collected Papers*, Cambridge, MA: Harvard University Press.

Rawls, John (2001), *Justice as Fairness: A Restatement*, E. Kelly (ed.), Cambridge, MA: Harvard University Press.

Ronzoni, Miriam (2009), 'The global order: a case of background injustice? A practice-dependent account', *Philosophy & Public Affairs* 37: 229–56.

Ronzoni, Miriam (2011), 'Life is not a camping trip: on the desirability of Cohenite socialism', *Politics, Philosophy & Economics* 11: 171–85.

Rorty, Richard (1991), *Objectivity, Relativism, and Truth: Philosophical Papers I*, Cambridge: Cambridge University Press.

Rossi, Enzo (2012), 'Justice, legitimacy and (normative) authority for political realists', *Critical Review of International Social and Political Philosophy* 15: 149–64.

Rossi, Enzo (2013), 'Consensus, compromise, justice and legitimacy', *Critical Review of International Social and Political Philosophy* 16: 557–72.

Rossi, Enzo and Matt Sleat (2014), 'Realism in normative political theory', *Philosophy Compass* 9: 689–701.

Rousseau, Jean-Jacques [1762] (1997), *The Social Contract and Other Later Political Writings*, V. Gourevitch (ed. and trans.), Cambridge: Cambridge University Press.

Sangiovanni, Andrea (2007), 'Global justice, reciprocity, and the state', *Philosophy & Public Affairs* 35: 3–39.

Sangiovanni, Andrea (2008), 'Justice and the priority of politics to morality', *The Journal of Political Philosophy* 16: 137–64.

Sangiovanni, Andrea (2011), 'Global justice and the morality of coercion, imposition, and framing,' in A. Banai, M. Ronzoni and C. Schemmel (eds), *Social Justice, Global Dynamics: Theoretical and Empirical Perspectives*, Routledge: London, pp. 26–45.

Sangiovanni, Andrea (2016), 'How practices matter', *The Journal of Political Philosophy* 24: 3–23.

Saunders, Ben (2011), 'Book review of Talisse's *Democracy and Moral Conflict*', *Mind* 120: 1312–15.

Sellars, Wilfrid [1956] (1997), *Empiricism and the Philosophy of Mind*, R. Brandom (ed.), Cambridge, MA: Harvard University Press.

Sepielli, Andrew (2009), 'What to do when you don't know what to do', in R. Shafer-Landau (ed.), *Oxford Studies in Metaethics: Volume 4*, Oxford: Oxford University Press, pp. 5–28.

Shapiro, Ian (1999), *Democratic Justice*, New Haven, CT: Yale University Press.

Simmons, John (2001), *Justification and Legitimacy: Essays on Rights and Obligations*, Cambridge: Cambridge University Press.

Simmons, John (2010), 'Ideal and nonideal theory', *Philosophy & Public Affairs* 38: 5–36.

Sleat, Matt (2009), 'Justification, pluralism and pragmatism: the problems and possibilities of a Peircian epistemic justification of liberalism', *European Journal of Pragmatism and American Philosophy* 2: 38–58.

Sleat, Matt (2010), 'Bernard Williams and the possibility of a realist political theory', *European Journal of Political Theory* 9: 485–503.

Sleat, Matt (2016), 'Realism, liberalism and non-ideal theory or, are there two ways to do realistic political theory?' *Political Studies* 64: 27–41.

Sleat, Matt (forthcoming), 'What is a political value? Political philosophy and fidelity to reality', *Social Philosophy & Policy*.

Southwood, Nicholas (2011), 'The moral/conventional distinction', *Mind* 120: 761–802.

Speaks, Jeff (2010), 'Theories of meaning', in E. N. Zalta (ed.), *The Stanford Encyclopedia of Philosophy*, <https://plato.stanford.edu/entries/meaning/> (last accessed 16 October 2017).

Springs, Jason (2009), '"Dismantling the master's house:" freedom as ethical practice in Brandom and Foucault', *Journal of Religious Ethics* 37: 419–48.

Stemplowska, Zofia (2008), 'What's ideal about ideal theory?' *Social Theory and Practice* 34: 319–40.

Swift, Adam (2008), 'The value of philosophy in nonideal circumstances', *Social Theory and Practice* 34: 363–87.

Talisse, Robert (2005), *Democracy after Liberalism*, New York: Routledge.

Talisse, Robert (2007), *A Pragmatist Philosophy of Democracy*, New York: Routledge.

Talisse, Robert (2009a), *Democracy and Moral Conflict*, New York: Cambridge University Press.

Talisse, Robert (2009b), 'Folk epistemology and the justification of democracy', in R. Geenens and R. Tinnevelt (eds), *Does Truth Matter? Democracy and Public Space*, New York: Springer, pp. 41–54.

Talisse, Robert (2010), 'Reply to Festenstein', *Contemporary Political Theory* 9: 45–9.

Talisse, Robert (2014) 'Pragmatist political philosophy', *Philosophy Compass* 9: 123–30.

Tersman, Folke (1993), *Reflective Equilibrium: An Essay in Moral Epistemology*, Stockholm: Almqvist & Wiksell.

Tersman, Folke (2006), *Moral Disagreement*, Cambridge: Cambridge University Press.

Tsai, George (2014), 'Rational persuasion as paternalism', *Philosophy & Public Affairs* 42:78–112.

Tully, James (1989), 'Wittgenstein and political philosophy: understanding practices of critical reflection,' *Political Theory* 17: 172–204.

Tully, James (2002), 'Political philosophy as a critical activity', *Political Theory* 30: 533–55.

Tully, James (2009), *Public Philosophy in a New Key I: Democracy and Civic Freedom*, Cambridge: Cambridge University Press.

Tully, James (2011), 'Dialogue', *Political Theory* 39: 145–60.

Valentini, Laura (2011), 'Global justice and practice-dependence: conventionalism, institutionalism, functionalism', *The Journal of Political Philosophy* 19: 399–418.

Valentini, Laura (2012), 'Ideal vs. non-ideal theory: a conceptual map', *Philosophy Compass* 7: 654–64.

Valentini, Laura (2017), 'The case for ideal theory', in C. Brown and R. Eckersley (eds), *The Oxford Handbook of International Political Theory*, Oxford: Oxford University Press.

Väyrynen, Pekka (2013), *The Lewd, the Rude and the Nasty: A Study of Thick Concepts in Ethics*, Oxford: Oxford University Press.

Walzer, Michael (1983), *Spheres of Justice*, New York: Basic Books.

Walzer, Michael (1987), *Interpretation and Social Criticism*, Cambridge, MA: Harvard University Press.

Wedgwood, Ralph (2001), 'Conceptual role semantics for moral terms', *Philosophical Review* 110: 1–30.

Wellman, Christopher (1996), 'Liberalism, Samaritanism, and political legitimacy', *Philosophy & Public Affairs* 25: 211–37.

Williams, Bernard (1985), *Ethics and the Limits of Philosophy*. Cambridge, MA: Harvard University Press.

Williams, Bernard (2005), *In the Beginning Was the Deed: Realism and Moralism in Political Argument*, Oxford: Princeton University Press.

Wittgenstein, Ludwig (1953), *Philosophical Investigations*, G. Anscombe and R. Rhees (eds), Oxford: Blackwell.

Wittgenstein, Ludwig (1979), *On Certainty*, Oxford: Blackwell.

Ypi, Lea (2008), 'Statist cosmopolitanism', *Journal of Political Philosophy* 16: 48–71.

INDEX

EU representative:
Easy Access System Europe
Mustamäe tee 50, 10621 Tallinn, Estonia
Gpsr.requests@easproject.com

www.ingramcontent.com/pod-product-compliance
Lightning Source LLC
Chambersburg PA
CBHW070343270326

41926CB00017B/3959